The abc
of
BASIC

AN INTRODUCTION TO PROGRAMMING
FOR LIBRARIANS

The abc
of

AN INTRODUCTION TO PROGRAMMING
FOR LIBRARIANS

Eric J Hunter MA FLA AMIET
Senior Lecturer, Liverpool Polytechnic

CLIVE BINGLEY **b** LONDON

Copyright © Eric Hunter 1982
Published by Clive Bingley Limited
16 Pembridge Road, London W11 3HL
and printed and bound in the UK by
Redwood Burn Limited, Trowbridge, Wiltshire

First published 1982

British Library Cataloguing in Publication Data

Hunter, Eric J.
    The abc of BASIC: an introduction to programming
    for librarians.
    1. Basic (Computer program language)
    I. Title
    001.64'24   QA76.73.B3

    ISBN 0-85157-355-X

Typeset by Allset in 11 on 12 point Baskerville and 10 on 12 point Univers

CONTENTS

Introduction   7

Author's note   9

Acknowledgements   10

PART ONE — Basic BASIC   11

First steps — input and output   13
*Summary to this point — Use of the return key
— System commands — Editing*

Remarks   25

Calculations   26

Decisions (conditions)   28

Loops   29
Nested loops

Subroutines   35
Invalid input — Summary to this point

Character strings   39
String functions

Dimensions   47
Sorting

Printing facilities   52
Summary to this point

Flowcharts   58

PART TWO — illustrative programs   65

Cataloguing simulation   67
*Character string array — Reading the data —
The menu — Subroutines: classified sort and
print out routine; alphabetical sort and print
out routine; search by class number or by
author's name — Returning to the menu —
The data — Program listing — The program
in operation — Further modification of the
program*

Library issue system simulation 91
Program listing — The program in operation —
Further modification of the program

Searching through a character string 104
Program listing — The program in operation —
Further modification of the program —
Modifying the cataloguing simulation
program to enable a search to be made in the
full author's surname

Appendix — Files 110
Final note 115
Index 117

INTRODUCTION

It comes as a surprise to many people to discover that, despite the computer's prodigious capabilities, to date it possesses no reasoning power. The computer simply does exactly as it is told, no more and no less. When telling it what to do, it is little use talking to it in English, or any other natural language; the computer will remain impassively 'silent' and inactive.

The computer is an electronic machine; in essence the only operation that it can perform is to recognize the difference between something which is there, such as an electrical pulse, and something which is not, rather like a person knowing whether a light is on or off. This situation can be represented by a '1' for 'on' and a '0' for 'off'. There are only two possibilities and the computer therefore operates in binary, or base two, mode. A binary coded instruction would appear as a pattern of 1's and 0's, eg:

```
00101000010
```

It is quite difficult to learn how to write such machine coded instructions, although, at one time, computer operators *had* to learn this language. Similarly, it is difficult to teach the computer English, which is very complex, with a vast number of words and many different methods of expression. What would a computer make of the sentences: 'Henry lost his head', or 'The elephant's trunk has grown two feet'?

A compromise appears to be the best solution. This compromise may be biased towards the binary language of the computer or towards the English language. Languages biased towards binary, or 'low-level' languages, need not concern us for the moment. The alternative 'high-level' languages use familiar English words combined with mathematical expressions or symbols. Like English, these languages require a grammar or syntax, which must be strictly adhered to. The nearer the language is to English, the easier and quicker it is to write instructions. On the other hand, the execution time then tends to be slower, for the instructions must be 'translated' into pure binary, within the machine, before the computer can interpret them correctly.

7

There are at present something over two hundred high-level languages in use[1] and the number is growing each year. The first successful language of this nature was FORTRAN (FORmula TRANslator), which was developed by IBM in the mid-1950s for use with sceintific formulae. This is still the most widely used scientific language.[2]

As applications of the computer spread into non-scientific fields, the need arose for different types of language more suited to business and commercial operations. COBOL (COmmon Business Oriented Language) has been the most successful of these.

The language to be dealt with in this book, BASIC, was one of the special, all-purpose languages developed for *interactive* work, where the programmer enters his instructions directly via the keyboard of an on-line terminal or microcomputer. Currently, BASIC is the most common 'resident' microcomputer language and it is likely to remain so in the foreseeable future, although certain microcomputers make additional provision for the use of other languages, eg PASCAL.[3]

BASIC stands for Beginners' All-purpose Symbolic Instruction Code. It was devised at Dartmouth College, New Hampshire, United States, in 1964, as a simple computer instruction language. It has been proved to be a good, easy, first language to learn.

1 Meek, Brian L and Fairthorne, Simon *Using computers* Ellis Horwood, 1977, p76.

2 *ibid*, p74.

3 PASCAL is a recently developed general purpose language which appears to be gaining in popularity.

AUTHOR'S NOTE

The computer can be instructed to perform many functions. It can, for instance, carry out complex mathematical calculations; it can handle graphics; it can even make sounds. It is also very useful for certain 'clerical' type operations. This text is concerned with the latter, particularly with character manipulation. It is non-mathematical and is primarily intended for librarians, information handlers, and others with similar interests. It should, however, also be of use to anyone requiring an elementary introduction to the BASIC language.

It is aimed at the complete beginner and the illustrative programs are therefore written for ease of understanding rather than for sophistication of content and programming technique.

The text was developed at the School of Librarianship and Information Studies, Liverpool Polytechnic for use in the teaching of Computer Studies during the first year of the BA Hons Librarianship Course.

ACKNOWLEDGMENTS

My thanks are due to my daughter Fiona and my colleague Joan Bibby for working through the text and for their helpful suggestions.

In addition, I am very grateful for the most useful advice and comment offered by Kevin Walsh, Head of Computer Services, Liverpool Polytechnic, who also read through the work in draft form.

The sections of the program written for use at West Suffolk College of Further Education are reproduced by kind permission of the Librarian, Robin Shreeve, and Michael Dean, Lecturer in Computing.

The illustration on p103 is reproduced by kind permission of the City Librarian, Bradford.

PART ONE   BASIC BASIC

FIRST STEPS – INPUT AND OUTPUT

In essence, a computer requires the following components: an *input* device, a *processing* unit and an *output* device. Data, or information, and instructions are fed into the computer via the input device and held in an immediate access store, which is closely associated with the processing unit. The latter enables the data to be manipulated according to the instructions supplied. The result of any process carried out within the computer can be seen via the output device. This basic computer 'configuration' can be illustrated diagrammatically thus:

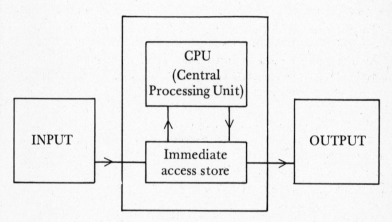

Where a microcomputer or a terminal (a means of communicating with a larger computer system) are concerned, the data and instructions are initially entered via a keyboard and the output is displayed on a v.d.u. (visual display unit). A printer may also be available for obtaining output on paper sheets or rolls. Some terminals employ a printer as an alternative to the v.d.u.

The keyboard of a microcomputer, or terminal, is rather like a typewriter keyboard and it is usually laid out and used in a similar way. There are, however, some differences. For example, the facility may exist for capital letters only. On the other hand, some additional characters or symbols, eg <, may be available.

Usually entries are made letter by letter, eg:

| P | R | I | N | T |

just as in typing but, on some microcomputers, one key may, in certain instances, represent a complete word, eg:

| PRINT |

Instructions and data cannot be kept permanently in an immediate access store. This is limited in capacity and, in a microcomputer, it must be cleared before a new set of instructions is entered. Some form of secondary, or backing store is therefore required. Magnetic tapes or magnetic disks, which can hold data in 'machine-readable' binary form, are used for this purpose. Instructions and data can thus be stored more permanently in this way and used as input whenever necessary.

As characters are 'typed', or keyed in, they appear on the screen of the v.d.u. and are subsequently transferred to the immediate access store (often referred to as the computer's 'memory'). Processed results are also displayed on the screen. The disk drives and printer are only brought into operation as necessary.

A set, or sequence of instructions telling the computer how to perform a particular task is known as a *program*. The words and symbols which are used to express the instructions make up the *programming language*.

The task to be performed must be broken down into a series of simple steps if the computer is to be able to understand what is required. In the BASIC programming language each step, each instruction, is called a *statement*.

In this first section of the text we shall examine how data and instructions are entered, or *input* to the computer, using BASIC, and also how data may be extracted, or *output*.

There are two words in the BASIC language for the input process:

INPUT   and   READ

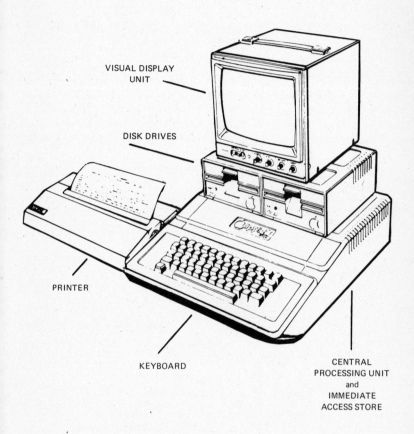

VISUAL DISPLAY
UNIT

DISK DRIVES

PRINTER

KEYBOARD

CENTRAL
PROCESSING UNIT
and
IMMEDIATE
ACCESS STORE

Figure 1 Typical microcomputer configuration.
The programs included in this text were tested
on such a system.

When information is to be extracted from the computer, or output, the relevant word in BASIC is:

PRINT

Suppose that we wish to enter into the computer's store a book's accession, or running number and its title. Here is a simple program, written in BASIC, and using the INPUT statement, which will enable this to be done. The programmer allocates names to the elements of data to be input so that the computer can keep track of them and so that they may be referred to again. These names must be selected in accordance with certain rules which will be explained at a later stage. The names selected, for use in this instance are 'N' for the accession number and 'T\$' for the title (the reason for the dollar sign will also become apparent later).

```
10    INPUT N
20    INPUT T$
30    END
```

Note that each statement in the program begins with a line number. The computer will carry out the instructions in the order of these numbers. The statements are numbered 10, 20, etc, rather than 1, 2, etc, so that further instructions may be interposed if desired, as the program is amended, modified and developed. Only capital letters are used; microcomputer implementations of BASIC are often restricted thus, but many library applications can still be handled quite adequately. After each complete statement has been entered and, indeed, after every command or piece of input, the Return key should be pressed. This acts as a signal for the computer to proceed. The termination of the program may be indicated by the statement END. As this program is entered via the keyboard it will appear on the v.d.u. screen.

The program is now held in the computer ready for use but the instructions contained in the program will not be carried out until the appropriate *command* is entered. The command required to operate a program is RUN.

```
RUN
?
```

The question mark, or prompt, which appears on the screen at this point (it may be a different symbol on some computers) informs the user that the computer is waiting for something to be entered. In this instance, in accordance with the first statement in the program, the computer is waiting for the user to enter, or input a number. Suppose that the accession number '1' is input:

```
RUN
?  1
```

The computer, following its instructions, will then expect a title and it will again prompt the user with a question mark. Suppose that the title *Great expectations* is now input:

```
?  GREAT EXPECTATIONS
```

So far so good, the information, or data, which consists of an accession number and a title, is now stored in the computer and is labelled so that it may be referred to again. If we wish to extract it, we simply use the appropriate output word, or statement, ie PRINT, and the names that we have allocated, ie PRINT N, T$. Here is the amended program with the additional statement interposed between lines 20 and 30:

```
   10    INPUT N
   20    INPUT T$
→ 25    PRINT N,T$
   30    END
```

When this amended program is operated, or RUN, and the information '1' and *Great expectations* is input, the computer will immediately respond by printing, on the screen:

```
1          GREAT EXPECTATIONS
```

Having run the program once, it could, if so desired, be run again. When this happens the data previously stored is deleted and new data can be entered if required, eg:

```
RUN
?  2
?  BLACK BEAUTY
```

17

with the result:

2   BLACK BEAUTY

This illustrates that the information, or data, to be input can be changed, ie it is *variable*. In the first 'RUN', N related to 1 and T$ to *Great expectations*. In the second 'RUN', N related to 2 and T$ to *Black Beauty*. N and T$ were, therefore, names of *variables*. The names of such variables must be selected in accordance with certain rules.

1 Names must *begin* with a letter.

2 Names of character variables must *end* with a dollar sign.

3 Names must not conflict with words which have a special meaning to the particular computer. These are known as *reserved* words.

Here are some sample names:

Numeric variables	*Character variables*
A	A$
B	B$
B2	CL$
SUM	DATE$
TOTAL	NAME$

or, as in the first illustrative example:

N   T$

The dollar sign informs the computer that the variable will contain characters. Each sequence of characters which is treated as a unit of information is known as a *string*. '*Great expectations*' and '*Black Beauty*' are strings.

It is sometimes useful to make names reflect the use to which they are being put. This gives them a mnemonic value. Take care, however, for the computer may utilize only part of the name, perhaps the first two letters, to distinguish one name from another. Thus RENT would therefore refer to the *same* variable as REPAYMENT.

Some computers continue to restrict names of variables to one letter. This therefore, will be the method adopted throughout the remainder of this text but remember that

18

such a restriction is becoming increasingly unusual and that longer names are permissible in many BASIC implementations.

The reader should now be able to:

i store information, or data, in the computer using the statement INPUT;

ii extract the data from the store and output it on to the v.d.u. screen using the statement PRINT.

The latter statement is extremely versatile. It can be used in a more direct way for including 'messages' within a program for printing on the screen. This facility can be used, for example, to provide explanations for the benefit of the *user* of the program. Our first program, for instance, might be amended to:

```
 5   PRINT "ENTER NUMBER"
10   INPUT N
15   PRINT "ENTER TITLE"
20   INPUT T$
25   PRINT N,T$
30   END
```

Any string of characters that is placed within inverted commas, or quotation marks, following the PRINT statement, is 'printed' on to the screen at the relevant point in the program. When the above program is put into operation, using th command RUN, the first instruction will be obeyed and o the v.d.u. screen will appear:

ENTER NUMBER
?

The number '1' might be entered as before and then

ENTER TITLE
?

will appear and '*Great expectations*' might be entered. The result will be the same as previously; the final output will be:

1   GREAT EXPECTATIONS

However, this time the computer 'explained' to the program user what sort of information was required.

19

It may be difficult to see, at this stage, why all information cannot be entered *directly*, eg '1 GREAT EXPECTATIONS', without going to the trouble of compiling a program. This will become clearer later. For the moment, it is sufficient to appreciate that a program enables us to:

(a) store data in the computer;
(b) label it so that it can be referred to again;
(c) output it as required.

The programs given above use the INPUT statement and the information, or data, was entered when the program was RUN.

It is possible to include the data *within* the program by making use of the READ statement. A READ statement must, however, always be coupled with a DATA statement. Here is a simple example:

```
10    READ N,T$
20    PRINT N,T$
30    DATA 1,"GREAT EXPECTATIONS"
40    END
```

When this program is RUN, a similar result to that obtained previously will be output:

```
1              GREAT EXPECTATIONS
```

The computer did not wait for information to be entered; it 'read' the information from the DATA statement whilst it was executing the program.

There can be more than one DATA statement but each must relate to a variable named in a READ statement. Examine the following program carefully.

```
10    READ N,T$,P,V$
20    PRINT N,T$
30    PRINT P,V$
40    DATA 1,"GREAT EXPECTATIONS"
50    DATA 2,"BLACK BEAUTY"
60    END
```

This program, when run, will print:

20

```
1        GREAT EXPECTATIONS
2        BLACK BEAUTY
```

The computer 'reads' the elements in order, so that variable
N related to 1, variable T$ relates to *Great expectations*,
variable P relates to 2 and variable V$ relates to *Black
Beauty*.

Note that character strings, when included in DATA
statements, are placed within quotation marks. Note also
that multiple DATA statements can appear on one numbered
'line', eg:

```
40    DATA 1,"GREAT EXPECTATIONS",2,"BLACK BEAUTY"
```

If headings are required, these can be printed as explained
on p19. The relevant additional statement is here shown
placed in the appropriate sequential position in the above
program by the numerical interposition facility mentioned
previously:

```
   10    READ N,T$,P,V$
→ 15    PRINT "NUMBER","TITLE"
   20    PRINT N,T$
   30    PRINT P,V$
   40    DATA 1,"GREAT EXPECTATIONS"
   50    DATA 2,"BLACK BEAUTY"
   60    END
```

When run, the result will be:

```
NUMBER  TITLE
1        GREAT EXPECTATIONS
2        BLACK BEAUTY
```

Summary to this point
A *program* consists of a sequence of instructions to a computer. Each instruction forms a *statement*. Each statement
begins with a *line number* and the program is executed in
the order of these numbers.

So far, the reader has been introduced to:

21

the input/output statements —

INPUT   allows user to enter data;

READ   allows data to be entered but must be combined with a DATA statement within the program. For each variable in the READ statement, there must be one item of information in the DATA statement(s);

PRINT   allows output and 'messages' to be printed;

the system command —

RUN   to execute the program; no line number is required;

and the statement —

END   which terminates a program. Very often the END statement is implicit and its omission will not prevent the running of a program. However, it does provide guidance where the understanding of a program is concerned.

The *variables* in a program are named for identification. Names must always begin with a letter and the names of character variables must end with a dollar sign.

Use of the Return key

A signal must be sent to the computer whenever the operator has finished a particular piece of input. The computer then knows that it is time to react. The usual way in which this is done is to press the Return key. Thus, this key is pressed every time that a line is completed, eg:

    10   PRINT "ENTER NUMBER"   [Return]

or after a system command, eg:

    RUN   [Return]

or after a particular piece of input, eg:

    ENTER TITLE
    ?   GREAT EXPECTATIONS   [Return]

System commands

At this stage, it is opportune to introduce the reader to several additional system commands which it is necessary to know when programming *interactively*, ie using a keyboard to communicate directly with the computer. We have already met the command RUN, which executes a program. Another essential command is:

LIST

This command causes the whole of the current program held in the computer's memory to be displayed on the screen or output to the printer. Sections of the program can normally be displayed by citing the particular lines required, eg:

LIST 100
LIST 100-200

A further essential command is:

NEW

which deletes the current program and all variables from the computer's memory and the user can then start afresh on a new program.

Certain commands which will be required if programs are to be stored on tape or disk include:

SAVE

which will cause the program currently held in the computer's memory to be stored on tape or disk, and:

LOAD*

which reads a program from tape or disk into the computer's memory ready for use.

The commands SAVE and LOAD are normally followed by the name allocated to the program, eg:

SAVE DATALIST

*This command may vary in some systems, for example, DEC BASIC would use the command OLD.

23

Editing

Note that instructions or data are not transmitted to the computer's memory until the Return key is pressed. If a v.d.u. (visual display unit) is being used, the screen will have a *cursor*, usually a 'blinking' square of light, which can be moved about the screen to positions where amendments may be required and characters can then be deleted or altered. It is thus quite easy to check and amend input before transmission to store.

It is just as easy to correct a program after input by referring to relevant line numbers. Complete lines can be deleted by simply typing the line number, eg:

100

and pressing the Return key. For deleting a group of lines the command DELete may be available, eg:

DEL 100-200

which deletes every statement between lines 100 and 200 inclusive.

If a line is to be replaced, simply type in the complete new line, eg:

100   PRINT "MAKE THIS A NEW LINE"

The programmer should make him or herself familiar with the editing and other facilities available on the particular machine in use.

REMARKS

It is extremely useful for the programmer, or the program user, to be able to read through a program and to understand it readily. A device which is of considerable assistance to this understanding is the REMARK or REM statement. Such statements can be inserted at any point in a program but the computer merely treats them as 'comments' and not as 'instructions'; it does not act upon them.

Here are a few examples of possible REM statements:

```
10    REM  PROGRAM  WRITTEN  BY  FIONA  HUNTER
20    REM  HISTOGRAM OF WORLD POPULATION
      EXPLOSION

 .  .  .

190   REM  YEAR IS FOLLOWED BY WORLD POPULATION
      IN MILLIONS
200   DATA "AD 1",250
210   DATA "1650",500
220   DATA "1750",750
```

As indicated, the REM statement can be used to cite the origin of a program, to name it, and to explain certain of its features.

CALCULATIONS

Although complex mathematical calculations are not the direct concern of the librarian or information specialist (and others working primarily with character strings), nevertheless it could well be advantageous for such persons to be able to program the computer to perform simple arithmetic operations. An obvious example, for instance, would be a count of the number of issues made from a library service point.

The word used in BASIC for any calculation is

LET

and the calculation is expressed as a formula using mathematical expressions or other symbols, eg:

LET C = A + B	ie A plus B
LET C = A - B	ie A minus B
LET C = A / B	ie A divided by B
LET C = A * B	ie A multiplied by B

Alternatively, the LET statement can be used to allocate a number to a variable, eg:

LET C = 1

Here is a simple program which will find the square of any number:

```
10    INPUT A
20    LET C = A * A
30    PRINT C
40    END
```

Here is the same program with a REM statement and some user guidance added:

```
4     REM   TO FIND THE SQUARE OF ANY NUMBER
7     PRINT "INPUT A NUMBER"
10    INPUT A
20    LET C = A * A
30    PRINT "THE SQUARE OF ";A;" = ";C
40    END
```

When this program is RUN, the computer will first print the instruction:

```
INPUT A NUMBER
?
```

Suppose that '9' is entered; the computer will then print:

```
THE SQUARE OF 9 = 81
```

Whenever the program is run, any number which is input will immediately be squared and the appropriate answer output.

In some versions of BASIC, the LET is implicit and may be omitted, eg:

```
10    INPUT A
20    C = A * A
30    PRINT C
40    END
```

The computer carries out calculations in a set order of priority, for example, multiplication and division will be done before addition and subtraction. Hence 2 + 6 * 7 would equal 44, ie 2 + (6 * 7), and *not* 56.

Most versions of BASIC also provide functions such as SIN, COS, TAN, EXP (exponentiation) etc and a RND function which will generate random numbers. The latter is useful for statistical purposes and for computer games, eg for dice throwing.

DECISIONS (CONDITIONS)

A fundamental requirement in programming is an ability to test whether a certain condition is fulfilled or not and, according to the answer, to take appropriate action. BASIC uses the

IF . . . THEN

statement for this purpose.

For example, it might be necessary to test the nature of the answer to a question and for the computer to respond accordingly, eg:

```
10    PRINT "IS SEWELL THE AUTHOR OF BLACK BEAUTY?"
20    PRINT "ANSWER YES OR NO"
30    INPUT A$
40    IF A$ = "YES" THEN GOTO 70
50    IF A$ = "NO" THEN PRINT "SORRY, YOU ARE WRONG"
60    GOTO 80
70    PRINT "GOOD, YOU ARE RIGHT"
80    END
```

The IF . . . THEN statement is often linked with a GOTO statement. The latter transfers the program sequence to another specified line number. The GOTO statement need not necessarily be used in conjunction with an IF . . . THEN statement; it can, of course, be used alone. However, its use in this way should be carefully watched for a program which continually switches from one place to another can be difficult to understand and to modify.

In fact, there is a more likely alternative to the GOTO statement which is used on line 60 of the above program, ie:

```
60    STOP
```

The STOP statement provides a means of halting the program at some point within it, in order to avoid a progression to instructions which are not required in a particular instance.

LOOPS

One of the great advantages of the computer is its ability to do things repeatedly, accurately and with unbelievable speed. When a particular section of a program is executed again and again then this is known as a *loop*.

A loop can be executed using the

GOTO

statement, which, as we have seen, transfers the program sequence to another specified line number, eg:

```
10    PRINT "HELLO"
20    GOTO 10
```

This program would, in theory, go on printing the word 'Hello' ad infinitum.

The number of times the loop is repeated could be governed by the inclusion in the program of a simple *count* mechanism, using the recently encountered LET statement, eg:

```
10    LET C = 0
20    PRINT "HELLO"
30    LET C = C + 1
40    IF  C < 20  THEN  GOTO 20       ie if C is less than 20
50    END
```

The count is 'initialized' in line 10. Every time 'Hello' is printed, '1' is added to the count (line 30). The IF . . . THEN condition statement in line 40 decides whether the correct number of loops has been executed, ie in this case, the correct number of 'Hello's' printed. This program would print 'Hello' twenty times.

It is rarely necessary to use the GOTO statement for loops, however, as there is a special facility built in to BASIC, which consists of the statements:

FOR   and   NEXT

Such a FOR . . . NEXT loop always begins with the word

29

FOR and always ends with the word NEXT. It contains a counter which controls the number of times an operation is to be repeated.

The above program might be written as:

```
10    FOR I = 1 TO 20
20    PRINT "HELLO"
30    NEXT I
40    END
```

Here is a loop which will READ three different numeric variables and three different character strings:

```
10    FOR I = 1 TO 3
20    READ N,T$
30    NEXT I
```

Here is a loop which will READ and PRINT the three numeric variables and the three character strings:

```
10    FOR I = 1 TO 3
20    READ N,T$
30    PRINT N,T$
40    NEXT I
```

There is only one READ statement and one PRINT statement but they will be repeated three times, so that there must be *three* corresponding DATA statements:

```
10    FOR I = 1 TO 3
20    READ N,T$
30    PRINT N,T$
40    NEXT I
50    DATA 1,"GREAT EXPECTATIONS"
60    DATA 2,"BLACK BEAUTY"
70    DATA 3,"LITTLE WOMEN"
80    END
```

When run, this program will achieve the result:

```
1          GREAT EXPECTATIONS
2          BLACK BEAUTY
3          LITTLE WOMEN
```

Note how the loop enables a number of *different* items of information to be referred to by the *one* variable name.

If headings are required, then these need only be printed once and the relevant instruction must, therefore, be *outside* the loop. The following statement could be added to the above program. The allocation of the line number '5' ensures that the instruction is in the correct operational sequence and that it is outside the loop.

```
5          PRINT "NUMBER","TITLE"
```

When the program is run, the result would now be:

```
NUMBER   TITLE
1          GREAT EXPECTATIONS
2          BLACK BEAUTY
3          LITTLE WOMEN
```

Nested loops
It is possible to place loops one inside the other. Such loops are called *nested* loops. Here is a fuller version of the program previously referred to which will print a histogram of the world population explosion:

```
10    REM   PROGRAM WRITTEN BY FIONA HUNTER
20    REM   HISTOGRAM OF WORLD POPULATION
      EXPLOSION
30    PRINT "WORLD POPULATION EXPLOSION"
40    PRINT
50    PRINT "YEAR","POPULATION"
60    PRINT
70    FOR J = 1 TO 12
80    READ Y$,P
90    PRINT Y$,
100   FOR K = 1 TO P/250
110   PRINT "+";
120   NEXT K
```

```
130    PRINT
140    NEXT J
150    PRINT
160    PRINT "+ = 250 MILLION"
170    PRINT
180    PRINT "1990 AND 2000 ARE ESTIMATED"
190    REM   YEAR IS FOLLOWED BY WORLD POPULATION
       IN MILLIONS
200    DATA "AD 1",250
210    DATA "1650",500
220    DATA "1750",750
230    DATA "1800",1000
240    DATA "1850",1250
250    DATA "1900",1500
260    DATA "1925",2000
270    DATA "1950",2500
280    DATA "1970",3500
290    DATA "1980",4500
300    DATA "1990",5500
310    DATA "2000",6500
320    END
```

The above program contains a nested loop. The outer loop, lines 70-140, reads the data and prints the dates. The inner loop, lines 100-120, prints a series of '+' signs to represent the population in a particular year. Each '+' equals 250 million people (note how, in line 100, each population in the data list is divided by 250 to give the correct number of '+'s).

Here is the result that would be obtained when this program is run. Note that a histogram printed by computer usually runs across the page rather than from top to bottom.

WORLD POPULATION EXPLOSION

YEAR	POPULATION
AD 1	+
1650	++
1750	+++
1800	++++
1850	+++++
1900	++++++
1925	+++++++
1950	+++++++++
1970	++++++++++++++
1980	+++++++++++++++++++
1990	++++++++++++++++++++++++
2000	+++++++++++++++++++++++++++++

+ = 250 MILLION

1990 AND 2000 ARE ESTIMATED

Care must be taken to ensure that loops are 'nested' correctly. The nested loops shown in diagrammatic form below are quite acceptable:

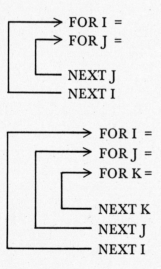

```
FOR I =
  FOR J =

  NEXT J
NEXT I


FOR I =
  FOR J =
    FOR K =

    NEXT K
  NEXT J
NEXT I
```

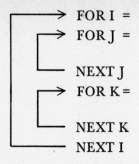

But such a nested loop as that shown in the next diagram is not acceptable and could cause major problems:

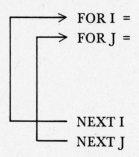

A nested loop would be required for an alphabetical sort program. A program of this nature will be described at a later point in this text.

SUBROUTINES

It could well be that a certain section of a program may be needed more than once. To save writing the section again and again, it can be placed in a *subroutine* and called up as required.

In BASIC, a subroutine is entered using the

GOSUB

statement and the

RETURN

statement is used to get back into the main stream of the program.

An example might be found in a 'quiz' program, eg:

```
10      PRINT "LITERATURE QUIZ"
20      PRINT "ANSWER EACH QUESTION TRUE (ENTER T)
        OR FALSE (ENTER F)"
30      PRINT "Q1  IS IT TRUE THAT SEWELL WROTE BLACK
        BEAUTY? "
40      GOSUB 1000
50      PRINT "Q2  IS IT TRUE . . .
60      GOSUB . . .
        . . .

1000    REM SUBROUTINE FOR TRUE AS RIGHT ANSWER
1010    INPUT A$
1020    IF A$ = "T" THEN GOTO 1050
1030    IF A$ = "F" THEN PRINT "SORRY, YOU ARE
        WRONG"
1040    GOTO 1060
1050    PRINT "GOOD, YOU ARE RIGHT"
1060    RETURN
```

Note that after a question is asked, the program switches to the subroutine for the answer to be entered and for a response to that answer to be given. The RETURN statement then takes the program back to print the next question. This subroutine could be used for any number of questions as long as 'True' is the right response. A second subroutine would cater for questions where 'False' was the correct answer.

Subroutines can also be useful when it is desired to provide the program user with a number of different options. For example, a search under authors' names could be covered by one subroutine and a search under classification numbers by another.

Invalid input

For simplicity of explanation, and because the reader's knowledge is not yet sufficiently advanced, no means of detecting and acting upon invalid input has been included in the above subroutine. It should, however, be stressed that this is most important. The program, as shown, does not print anything if neither 'T' nor 'F' is entered by the user. A wrong key can easily be pressed by mistake. In practice, a test would be included for this and if A$ did not equal 'T' or 'F' then appropriate action would be taken and the user given further instruction. This point will be explained in more detail later in this text.

Summary to this point

So far, the reader has been introduced to the following BASIC statements:

END	terminates a program;
FOR . . . NEXT	permits a loop to be executed which performs the operation between the FOR statement and the NEXT statement a specified number of times;
GOSUB	causes the program to *branch* to a specified line number which begins a subroutine. The subroutine ends with a RETURN statement which transfers the program back to the statement immediately following the GOSUB command;

GOTO	causes the program to branch to a specified line number;
IF . . . THEN	causes the program to test for a particular condition and to make a decision about whether to take a particular action or jump to a specified line number;
INPUT	allows the user to enter data;
LET	assigns a new value to a variable within the program;
PRINT	allows output and 'messages' to be printed;
READ	allows data to be entered but must be combined with a DATA statement within the program. For each variable in the READ statement, there must be one item of information in the DATA statement(s). In both READ and DATA statements, variables or items of information must be separated by commas. In DATA statements items of information which consist of character strings must be in inverted commas;
REM	allows comments to be inserted in a program. These are ignored by the computer;
STOP	allows the program to be halted at a specified point.

To execute the program, the system command is:

RUN

To cause the whole of the current program held in the computer's memory to be displayed on the screen or output to the printer, the system command is:

LIST

Sections of the program can be displayed by citing the particular lines required:

```
LIST 30
LIST 30-80
```

Sections of the program may be deleted by the DELete command:

```
DEL   100-200
```

The command:

```
NEW
```

deletes the current program and all variables from the computer's memory.

A program can be stored on tape or disk by using the command:

```
SAVE
```

and the command:

```
LOAD
```

reads a program from tape or disk into the computer's memory ready for use.

CHARACTER STRINGS

For computer applications in libraries and information services, the manipulation of strings of alphabetic and numeric characters is of prime importance. It must be possible, for instance, to sort characters into alphabetic and other orders and an ability to search for particular strings is also vital.

As indicated previously, a string is a sequence of characters. The string may include not only alphabetic characters but also numeric characters, spaces and punctuation marks. It is important to remember that a computer cannot 'read', in the accepted sense; a space is a 'character' to the computer.

Here are some examples of strings of characters:

ABC	(String contains 3 characters)
JOE SOAP	(String contains 8 characters)
SOAP, JOE	(String contains 9 characters)
THE ODESSA FILE	(String contains 15 characters)
PR 2832	(String contains 7 characters)

The number of characters in a string may be of great significance as will be seen later.

Useful operations involving character strings can be performed by many of the BASIC statements. Some of these operations have already been described. We have seen, for instance, how the INPUT, READ, PRINT and DATA statements might be used and we have seen that names ending in a dollar sign are reserved for string variables.

The following program contains PRINT and INPUT statements, includes four string constants, eg 'Hello, I am a computer', and one string variable, N$, which will relate to the name of the program user.

```
10    PRINT "HELLO, I AM A COMPUTER"
20    PRINT "WHAT IS YOUR NAME? "
30    INPUT N$
40    PRINT "HELLO ";N$;" I AM PLEASED TO MEET YOU"
50    END
```

The LET statement can also be utilized. The above program might be changed to:

```
10    LET A$ = "HELLO"
20    PRINT A$;", I AM A COMPUTER"
30    PRINT "WHAT IS YOUR NAME? "
40    INPUT N$
50    PRINT A$;" ";N$;" I AM PLEASED TO MEET YOU"
```

Note particularly the way that a comma and space are placed after the 'Hello' in line 20 and the way in which a space is 'printed' between the 'Hello' and the user's name in line 50. The use of the semi-colon is also important. This ensures that the print head is kept on the one line and that each element on the one line follows on directly. This will be explained in more detail in a future section.

An instruction such as

```
10    LET X$ = Y$
```

is also valid. For example, the program:

```
10    LET Y$ = "GOOD MORNING"
20    LET X$ = Y$
30    PRINT X$
40    END
```

would result in the printing of the message "Good morning".

Some versions of BASIC allow a null string, which contains no characters and which can be set up thus:

```
10    LET R$ = ""
```

The IF . . . THEN statement is a powerful tool where the manipulation of character strings is concerned. We shall see later how it may be used in searches for specific strings, eg:

If N$ = "DICKENS" THEN . . .

Here is an example of how an IF . . . THEN statement might be used to escape from a loop when required.

```
10    FOR K = 1 TO 50
20    INPUT A$
30    IF A$ = "ZZZ" THEN 50
40    NEXT K
50    END
```

The above program would allow up to fifty string variables to be input. If, at any time, 'ZZZ' is entered as the variable, then the program is transferred to a line number outside the loop. This is a very useful facility. The characters chosen as the 'escape' string must constitute a 'rogue' string, ie one that is unlikely to occur in normal circumstances.

The IF . . . THEN statement can, in fact, be used with other relational operators, eg:

IF A$ < B$ THEN . . .	Means if the string A$ is less than the string B$
IF A$ > B$ THEN . . .	Means if the string A$ is greater than the string B$
IF "JONES" < B$ THEN . . .	Means if the string "JONES" is less than B$
IF A$ < = B$ THEN . . .	Means if the string A$ is less than or equal to B$

The question is, of course, how does the computer know whether one string is of greater or lesser value than another and, even if it does know, what use can that knowledge be?

The answer to this question is the secret of the way in which alphabetical sorting can be done by the machine. Every character has a predetermined value allocated to it within the computer. A is less value than B, B is less value than C, C is less value than D, and so on through the alphabet. Other examples are:

ABC is greater than ABB
ABC is less than ABD
JONES is less than SMITH
JONES is greater than BROWN
JONES is greater than JOHNSON

41

Numerals have less value than letters; punctuation marks have various values; a space has the least value of all.

One of the most common ways of ranking characters is by the use of the standard ASCII (American Standard Code for Information Interchange) character set, although this is not used in all microcomputers.

String functions

Certain predefined string functions are provided in BASIC which are very helpful in string manipulation. For example, the number of characters in a string can be counted, or a string can be broken down into parts, or a string can be 'searched' to see if it contains another string, and so on.

Some examples follow, although it should be noted that all of these may not be present in certain versions of BASIC and, in other versions, they may be referred to by different names.

CHR$(N) This function gives the character whose numeric code is N. Using ASCII CHR$(65) = "A".

LEN(A$) Gives the number of characters in the string A$. LEN("BASIC") = 5

A sample program would be:

```
10   LET A$ = "GOOD MORNING"
20   PRINT LEN(A$)
30   END

RUN
12
```

LEFT$(A$,N) Refers to the first N characters of the string A$, eg:

```
10   LET A$ = "GOOD MORNING"
20   PRINT LEFT$(A$,3)
30   END

RUN
GOO
```

42

RIGHT$(A$,N)   Refers to the last N characters of the
               string A$, eg:

```
10    Let A$ = "GOOD MORNING"
20    PRINT RIGHT$(A$,3)
30    END
```

```
RUN
ING
```

MID$(A$,N)   Refers to that part of the string A$
               beginning at the Nth character, eg:

```
10    LET A$ = "GOOD MORNING"
20    PRINT MID$(A$,6)
30    END
```

```
RUN
MORNING
```

MID$(A$,N,P)   Refers to that part of the string A$
               beginning at the Nth character and
               continuing for P characters, eg:

```
10    LET A$ = "GOOD MORNING"
20    PRINT MID$(A$,6,4)
30    END
```

```
RUN
MORN
```

STR$(N)   Returns a string that is a character
               representation of a numeric expres-
               sion, eg:

```
10    LET N = 4.2
20    PRINT STR$(N)
```

```
RUN
4.2
```

Code	Character	Code	Character
32		64	@
33	!	65	A
34	"	66	B
35	#	67	C
36	$	68	D
37	%	69	E
38	&	70	F
39	'	71	G
40	(	72	H
41	)	73	I
42	*	74	J
43	+	75	K
44	,	76	L
45	—	77	M
46	.	78	N
47	/	79	O
48	0	80	P
49	1	81	Q
50	2	82	R
51	3	83	S
52	4	84	T
53	5	85	U
54	6	86	V
55	7	87	W
56	8	88	X
57	9	89	Y
58	:	90	Z
59	;	91	[
60	<	92	\
61	=	93	]
62	>	94	∧
63	?	95	—

Figure 2 ASCII Character set — the printable ASCII characters with their decimal codes. (Note that many BASIC implementations using ASCII characters will also handle lower case. Lower case letters are represented by ASCII codes 97 to 122)

VAL(A$)	The reverse of STR$. It returns the VALue of the contents of a string, rather than its actual contents, eg:

```
10    LET A$ = "13"
20    PRINT VAL(A$)

RUN
13
```

The VAL statement helps to alleviate the problems which may arise because of the fact that character strings, although they may include numbers, cannot be interpreted arithmetically.

Here is an example of how a string function might be used;

```
10    INPUT A$
20    IF LEFT$(A$,4) = "THE " THEN GOTO 50
30    PRINT A$
40    STOP
50    PRINT MID$(A$,5);",  THE"
60    END
```

In this program, if the string which is input begins with "THE ", then the string is inverted so that ", THE" is printed at the end. Any string which does not begin with "THE " is printed as it stands. Indicated below is the result of running the program twice, first with the input 'DAILY MAIL' and then with the input 'THE GUARDIAN'.

```
RUN
?  DAILY MAIL
DAILY MAIL

RUN
?  THE GUARDIAN
GUARDIAN, THE
```

Note the way a STOP is used in this program to prevent both PRINT statements being executed.

Where string functions are concerned, the manual for the particular computer in use should be examined in order to ascertain the facilities offered.

DIMENSIONS

To be limited to the names A$ to Z$ for character string variables would be inhibiting and frustrating. Fortunately, it is possible to set up 'arrays' of strings by the use of the DIM (dimension) statement. This sets up a list of variables under only one name. For example:

A$(10)

refers to a list of ten character strings: A$(1), A$(2), A$(3), and so on to A$(10). A$(1) might be *Great expectations*, A$(2) *Black Beauty*, A$(3) *Little women* etc.

The 'subscript', in the above instance any number from 1 to 10, can also be an expression, eg A$(J) refers to the Jth entry in the list A$; A$(J+1) refers to the entry following A$(J).

Lists can, of course, also be set up for numeric variables. N(4) would refer to the fourth numeric variable in the list N.

The DIM statement specifies the size of lists, for example the statement

```
10    DIM N(500),T$(500)
```

would set up two lists, one of up to five hundred numeric variables and the other of up to five hundred string variables.

The following program illustrates the use of the DIM statement:

```
10    DIM N(4),T$(4)
20    READ N(1),T$(1),N(2),T$(2),N(3),T$(3),N(4),T$(4)
30    PRINT "NUMBER","TITLE"
40    PRINT
50    PRINT N(1),T$(1)
60    PRINT N(2),T$(2)
70    PRINT N(3),T$(3)
80    PRINT N(4),T$(4)
90    DATA 1,"GREAT EXPECTATIONS"
100   DATA 2,"BLACK BEAUTY"
110   DATA 3,"LITTLE WOMEN"
120   DATA 4,"TREASURE ISLAND"
130   END
```

When run, the result of this program will be:

NUMBER	TITLE
1	GREAT EXPECTATIONS
2	BLACK BEAUTY
3	LITTLE WOMEN
4	TREASURE ISLAND

This is obviously an improvement upon the procedure employed in previous programs which required different variable names for each of the data elements. In addition, this program would not restrict the number of such elements. However, it is a rather long-winded way of writing the program; the use of a loop would prove more economical.

```
10    DIM N(4),T$(4)
20    PRINT "NUMBER","TITLE"
30    PRINT
40    FOR I = 1 TO 4
50    READ N(I),T$(I)
60    PRINT N(I),T$(I)
70    NEXT I
80    DATA 1,"GREAT EXPECTATIONS"
90    DATA 2,"BLACK BEAUTY"
100   DATA 3,"LITTLE WOMEN"
110   DATA 4,"TREASURE ISLAND"
120   END
```

A close study of these two programs will reveal that they achieve the same result. The variable names being N(1) to N(4) and T$(1) to T$(4) in both cases.

Sorting

Amongst many other operations, the use of the DIM statement and the fact that the subscript can be any expression facilitates sorting procedures. Sorting can be carried out in different ways. One of the most common in the 'bubble' sort, in which the highest or the lowest numbers, or 'values' of characters, rise to the top like bubbles in a liquid.

48

Each variable in a list is compared with the next. If they are in the right order they are left undisturbed but if in the wrong order they are interchanged. This process continues until the correct ascending or descending order is achieved.

The following program enables a list of variable character strings to be entered. The number of strings is pre-selected and input by the person running the program. The character strings are then entered one by one and, after the last string has been input, the program automatically sorts the strings into alphabetical order.

```
10    INPUT N
20    DIM A$(N)
30    FOR I = 1 TO N
40    INPUT A$(I)
50    NEXT I
60    FOR J = 1 TO N − 1
70    FOR K = 1 TO N − 1
80    IF A$(K) < A$(K+1) THEN GOTO 120
90    LET X$ = A$(K)
100   LET A$(K) = A$(K+1)
110   LET A$(K+1) = X$
120   NEXT K
130   NEXT J
140   HOME
150   PRINT "ALPHABETICAL LISTING"
160   PRINT
170   FOR L = 1 TO N
180   PRINT A$(L)
190   NEXT L
200   END
```

When the program is run, the computer will first wait for a number to be entered (N). If the number 6 is input then the computer will set up a list of six character variables (line 20), A$(1) to A$(6). It will then wait for this list to be filled (lines 30-50). The remainder of the program sorts the list and prints it out in the required order.

The hub of the program is contained in the lines 60 to 130. The inner loop 70-120 performs one 'pass' through the list,

49

interchanging strings if they are not in alphabetical order. At the end of the first pass, the last item must be the string nearest the end of the alphabet. At the end of the second pass, the next to last item must be the next to last in alphabetical order. This process continues until the correct order is achieved. The outer loop 60-130 controls the number of passes through the list. The number of 'comparisons' in each pass must obviously equal one less than the number of strings to be sorted, ie N-1. The number of passes that might be necessary will vary according to the original order but the maximum number will be the number required when the order is the complete reverse of that required. This will also equal N-1.

This is the sequence in which the sorting would be done for the six character strings shown:

Original order of input	*First pass*
GREAT EXPECTATIONS	BLACK BEAUTY
BLACK BEAUTY	GREAT EXPECTATIONS
LITTLE WOMEN	LITTLE WOMEN
TREASURE ISLAND	ROBINSON CRUSOE
ROBINSON CRUSOE	GULLIVER'S TRAVELS
GULLIVER'S TRAVELS	TREASURE ISLAND

Second pass	*Third pass*
BLACK BEAUTY	BLACK BEAUTY
GREAT EXPECTATIONS	GREAT EXPECTATIONS
LITTLE WOMEN	GULLIVER'S TRAVELS
GULLIVER'S TRAVELS	LITTLE WOMEN
ROBINSON CRUSOE	ROBINSON CRUSOE
TREASURE ISLAND	TREASURE ISLAND

This sort program introduces a new statement —

HOME

This statement clears the screen so that only the alphabetical listing will be seen when the run is complete. This statement may vary in different versions of BASIC, eg CLS (clear screen).

50

The program could be improved by including operator instructions to be printed on the screen, eg:

```
5    PRINT"ENTER THE NUMBER OF ITEMS TO BE SORTED"

25   PRINT "ENTER ";N;" ITEMS"
```

It should also be noted that although it is here presented as a program for sorting alphabetically, it can be used to sort numerically or alphanumerically without amendment.

An input such as:	would be sorted into:
136	025
822	136
745	745
942	822
025	942

and an input such as:	would be sorted into:
PR 8233	HE 4521
HE 6933	HE 6933
TF 1357	MF 2635
MF 2635	PR 8233
HE 4521	TF 1357

Using character string variables for sorting classification numbers is useful to the librarian because it permits a number beginning with '0' to be printed. In normal circumstances, using numeric variables, the computer would print 025 simply as 25, the leading zero being meaningless.

PRINTING FACILITIES

So that output may be 'laid out' in an appropriate manner, it is necessary for the programmer to be aware of the printing facilities available and of the restrictions which may be imposed.

The length of a permissible line will depend upon the equipment in use. For example, a typical v.d.u. screen might be limited to 80 characters or, on a smaller microcomputer, 40 characters. A printer will allow a longer line, usually 120/132 characters or, on a smaller printer, 80 characters. On a screen there is also an obvious limit to the number of lines which can be displayed at one time, 24 being a typical number.

The following three programs illustrate how various layouts may be obtained. The programs look very much the same but, in fact, each will achieve a different result.

```
10    FOR J = 1 TO 15
20    PRINT "HELLO"
30    NEXT J
40    END

10    FOR J = 1 TO 15
20    PRINT "HELLO";
30    NEXT J
40    END

10    FOR J = 1 TO 15
20    PRINT "HELLO",
30    NEXT J
40    END
```

Each program uses a loop to print the word 'Hello' fifteen times.

The first program will print a series of 'Hello's in a vertical column on the left hand side:

```
HELLO
HELLO
```

```
HELLO
HELLO
HELLO
HELLO
HELLO
HELLO
HELLO
HELLO
HELLO
HELLO
HELLO
HELLO
HELLO
```

The second program will print the 'Hello's horizontally one after the other usually with no spacing between:

```
HELLOHELLOHELLOHELLOHELLOHELLOHELLOHELLO
HELLOHELLOHELLOHELLOHELLOHELLOHELLO
```

The third program will print a series of 'Hello's in columns, each 'Hello' on the one line being separated by a number of spaces:

```
HELLO          HELLO          HELLO
HELLO          HELLO          HELLO
HELLO          HELLO          HELLO
HELLO          HELLO          HELLO
HELLO          HELLO          HELLO
```

The number of columns is dependent upon screen width. It is normally five or, on a smaller microcomputer, three.

The first program shows that the computer will print consecutively in a vertical direction unless otherwise instructed.

The addition of a semi-colon in the second program holds the print head on the same line so that the computer will print consecutively in a horizontal direction.

In the third program, the semi-colon has been replaced by a comma. In all BASIC implementations the screen is divided into a series of 'zones'. The use of the comma performs the

53

special function of taking the print head out of one zone into the next, allowing the output to be printed in columns.

The printing of information in certain positions may also be achieved by the setting of tabs, just as on a typewriter. The statement

```
10    PRINT TAB(17) "HELLO"
```

will print 'Hello' in the centre of the screen, ie beginning in the seventeenth character position.

The statement

```
10    PRINT "                HELLO"
```

will print sixteen blank spaces before 'Hello' and will have a similar effect.

Some computers allow both HTAB's (horizontal tabs) and VTAB's (vertical tabs) to be set.

It should be noted that the PRINT statement alone will print a blank line. For example, the program

```
10    PRINT "NUMBER","TITLE"
20    PRINT
30    PRINT "1", "GREAT EXPECTATIONS"
40    END
```

would enable a blank line to be inserted between the heading and the entries, ie:

```
NUMBER  TITLE

1          GREAT EXPECTATIONS
```

An example of how printing facilities may be used can be found in the production of a 'standard' entry which requires a predetermined layout and punctuation. All of the punctuation and the layout can be included in the program and automatically produced by the computer.

If the detail in the entry relates to a sound recording, the input section of the program might appear as:

```
10    REM PRINT OUT OF STANDARD ENTRY
20    PRINT "ENTER COMPOSER'S SURNAME"
```

```
 30    INPUT N$
 40    PRINT "ENTER COMPOSER'S FORENAME"
 50    INPUT F$
 60    PRINT "ENTER TITLE"
 70    INPUT T$
 80    PRINT "ENTER RECORD PUBLISHER"
 90    INPUT P$
100    PRINT "ENTER DATE"
110    INPUT D$
120    PRINT "ENTER SPEED IN RPM"
130    INPUT R
140    PRINT "ENTER STEREO OR MONO"
150    INPUT M$
160    PRINT "ENTER PERFORMER"
170    INPUT E$
180    PRINT "ENTER RECORD NO"
190    INPUT B$
200    PRINT "ENTER CLASS NO"
210    INPUT C$
```

and the output section as:

```
220    PRINT N$;", ";F$
230    PRINT TAB(4) T$;". - "
240    PRINT P$;", ";D$;"."
250    PRINT TAB(4) "SOUND RECORDING : ";R;"RPM,
       ";M$;"."
260    PRINT TAB(4) "PERFORMED BY ";E$;"."
270    PRINT TAB(4) P$;" ";B$;"."
280    PRINT
290    PRINT TAB(30) C$
300    END
```

If the information input when the program was run were:

ENTER COMPOSER'S SURNAME	KHACHATURIAN
ENTER COMPOSER'S FORENAME	ARAM
ENTER TITLE	THE 'ONEDIN LINE' THEME

ENTER RECORD PUBLISHER	DECCA
ENTER DATE	1971
ENTER SPEED IN RPM	45
ENTER STEREO OR MONO	STEREO
ENTER PERFORMER	VIENNA PHILHARMONIC ORCH
ENTER RECORD NUMBER	F 13259
ENTER CLASS NUMBER	780

then the following entry would be produced by the program:

KHACHATURIAN, ARAM
    THE 'ONEDIN LINE' THEME. —
DECCA, 1971.
    SOUND RECORDING : 45RPM, STEREO.
    PERFORMED BY VIENNA PHILHARMONIC ORCH.
    DECCA F 13259.
              780

The program illustrates how an entry can be printed without the clerical chore of remembering, and inserting, the layout and punctuation. Once the necessary details are recorded in a program, then the computer will reproduce them once, twice, or a thousand times absolutely accurately.

Summary to this point
The following BASIC statements were defined in the previous summary on p36:

    END
    FOR . . . NEXT
    GOSUB
    GOTO
    IF . . . THEN
    INPUT
    LET

```
PRINT
READ
REM
STOP
```

To these may now be added:

DIM   a dimension statement which specifies the size of a list of information to be stored in one variable;

HOME   a statement which clears the screen and returns the cursor to the top left hand corner. Term may vary in some computers, eg CLS.

The following statement has not been used in this text but it could prove useful in certain circumstances:

RESTORE   this statement enables information in data statements to be used more than once during the running of a program. The instruction sends the computer back to the first data item.

The following commands were also defined on pp 37-38:

```
DEL
LIST
LOAD
NEW
RUN
SAVE
```

FLOWCHARTS

A diagrammatic representation of the steps involved in a computer program and the sequence in which they are to be carried out is known as a *flowchart*. Flowcharts can be of help to the programmer in planning his work and they can also assist in the clarification of complex programs. Flowcharts make it easier to break down an operation into its component elements and to identify the order of these elements correctly.

Here are a few sample flowcharts for programs already described in this text:

Flowchart example 1 (see p17)

Associated program

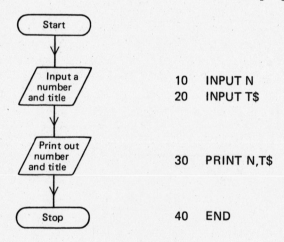

10	INPUT N
20	INPUT T$
30	PRINT N,T$
40	END

Flowchart example 2 (*see p27*)

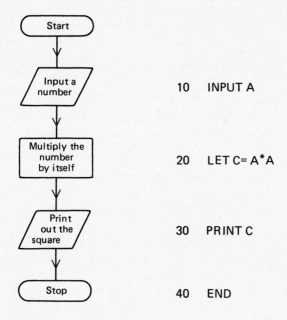

10	INPUT A
20	LET C= A*A
30	PRINT C
40	END

Flowchart example 3 (see p29)

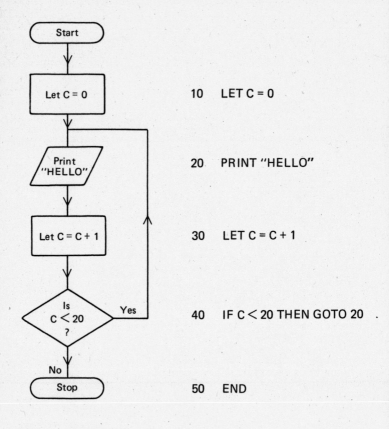

Flowchart	Program
Start	
Let C = 0	10 LET C = 0
Print "HELLO"	20 PRINT "HELLO"
Let C = C + 1	30 LET C = C + 1
Is C < 20 ? Yes	40 IF C < 20 THEN GOTO 20
No Stop	50 END

NB An alternative and more probable version of this program is:

```
10    FOR C = 1 TO 20
20    PRINT "HELLO"
30    NEXT C
40    END
```

Flowchart example 4 (see p45)

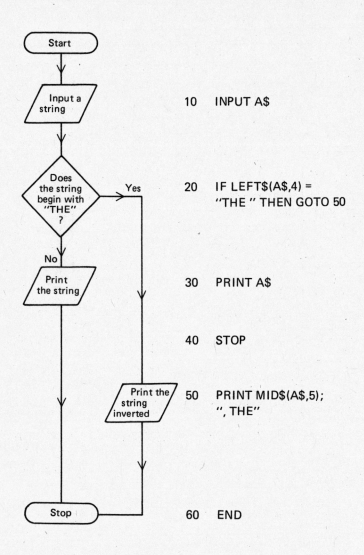

```
10    INPUT A$

20    IF LEFT$(A$,4) =
      "THE " THEN GOTO 50

30    PRINT A$

40    STOP

50    PRINT MID$(A$,5);
      ", THE"

60    END
```

Flowchart example 5 (*see p41*)

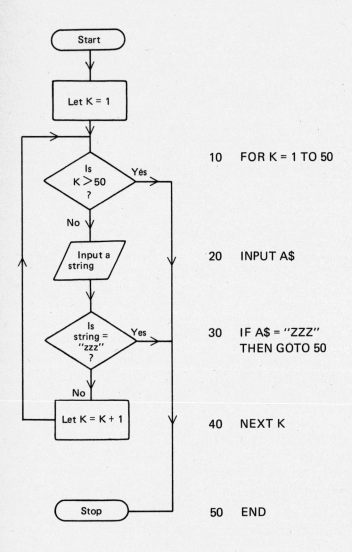

10	FOR K = 1 TO 50
20	INPUT A$
30	IF A$ = "ZZZ" THEN GOTO 50
40	NEXT K
50	END

The flowcharts illustrated depict the shapes of some of the 'boxes' in which the steps of a flowchart are written:

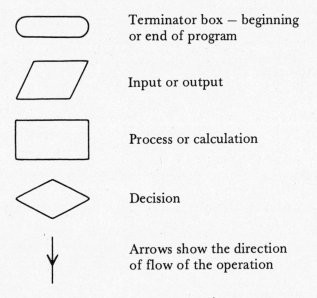

Terminator box — beginning or end of program

Input or output

Process or calculation

Decision

Arrows show the direction of flow of the operation

Flowchart symbols are standardized in British Standard BS 4058. Here are some further examples:

An input function in which the information is entered manually at the time of processing, eg by means of on-line keyboards.

An input/output function utilizing any type of on-line storage, eg magnetic tape, or magnetic disk.

An input/output function in which the medium is magnetic tape.

An input/output function in which the medium is a magnetic disk.

An input/output function in which the medium is a document.

The standard itself should be examined for a full list of the thirty basic symbols specified for use in flowcharts.

Whether a programmer uses the flowchart or not is a personal decision. Many programmers find them to be of great assistance but, in my experience, other programmers consider them superfluous and unnecessary. However, there is no doubt that problems which, at first sight seem trivial, can prove to be very complex and a pictorial representation may well be the best way to proceed at the planning stage of a program. Indeed, the use of flowcharts is now widespread outside the computer world as a means of simple explanation of particular processes.

64

PART TWO ILLUSTRATIVE PROGRAMS

The illustrative programs listed in the first part of this work were mainly quite short in length and mostly of no real practical value. In this second part, three further illustrative programs will be developed, using the principles described in Part 1, which will be somewhat more complex in nature. Hopefully, these programs will indicate more clearly how the knowledge acquired so far can be applied.

CATALOGUING SIMULATION

The first of these programs is one which enables a catalogue to be set up, in this case a list of books. The catalogue can then:

1 be printed out in alphabetical order;
2 be printed out in classified order;
3 be searched by author;
4 be searched by class number.

Character string array

The first step is to denote an array of character strings for each required element. The proposed catalogue is to contain the classification number, author's name, title and date of publication of each book. The maximum number of items to be catered for, in this instance, is to be fixed at one hundred, although this would vary according to the needs of the particular individual or institution and would be influenced by the storage capacity of the particular computer. The necessary statement is therefore:

```
10    DIM C$(100),N$(100),T$(100),D$(100)
```

The classification number, using certain classification schemes, could be purely numeric. The date of publication is also purely numeric. However, these two elements have been denoted here as character string variables rather than numeric variables. There are advantages in this where sorting (see p51) and searching are concerned. In this DIM statement, C$ relates to the classification number, N$ relates to the name of the author, T$ relates to the title and D$ relates to the date of publication. The chosen names of these variables are mnemonic, eg:

C$ = Classification number

Reading the data

The data to be input must be read and a loop can be used to do this. The number of times the loop is to be repeated must relate to the number of strings set up in the DIM statement:

67

```
11    FOR I = 1 TO 100
12    READ C$(I),N$(I),T$(I),D$(I)
18    NEXT I
```

There may not be a full 100 items in the catalogue at a given time and an avenue of escape from the loop must be supplied to cater for this. This is done by means of a 'rogue' string, ie:

```
14    IF C$(I) = "END  "THEN GOTO . . .
```

As the classification number (C$) is to consist of numeric digits, 'END' cannot conflict with a bona fide number.

If the number of items is less than one hundred, it will be necessary to ascertain exactly how many there are for reasons which will become apparent later. A count can be inserted for this purpose:

```
7     LET T = 0
12    READ C$(I),N$(I),T$(I),D$(I)
16    LET T = T + 1
```

This will add '1' to the count every time the data relating to an item is read.

The program, as so far written, will now appear as follows. A REM statement, giving the title of the program, has been added:

```
5     REM  CATALOGUING SIMULATION
7     LET T = 0
10    DIM C$(100),N$(100),T$(100),D$(100)
11    FOR I = 1 TO 100
12    READ C$(I),N$(I),T$(I),D$(I)
14    IF C$(I) = "END    " THEN GOTO 20
16    LET T = T + 1
18    NEXT I
20    HOME
```

The HOME statement (line 20) clears the screen ready for the next operation.

The menu
As there is to be a choice of various options, these must be printed on to the screen so that the user is able to select
68

the one that he or she might require. This, in computer parlance, is called a *menu*. This will be a *menu-driven* program.

Each option is numbered and the user is requested to enter the number corresponding to the function that is required:

```
30    PRINT TAB(9) "CATALOGUING SIMULATION"
40    PRINT
50    FOR A = 1 TO 40
60    PRINT "*";
70    NEXT A
80    PRINT : PRINT
90    PRINT "DO YOU REQUIRE:"
100   PRINT : PRINT TAB(8) "1  CLASSIFIED PRINT OUT"
110   PRINT TAB(8) "2  ALPHABETICAL PRINT OUT"
120   PRINT TAB(8) "3  SEARCH BY CLASS NO"
130   PRINT TAB(8) "4  SEARCH BY AUTHOR"
135   PRINT TAB(8) "5  EXIT THIS PROGRAM"
140   PRINT : PRINT
150   INPUT "ENTER APPROPRIATE NUMBER "; A
```

There are a number of features in this section of the program which require further explanation. Line 30 prints a heading starting at tab(9), ie in the centre of the screen. Line 40 'prints' a blank line. Lines 50 to 70 constitute a loop which prints a row of forty asterisks straight across the screen, in effect 'underlining' the heading. Line 80 'prints' two blank lines. Note that some versions of BASIC permit more than one statement with a single line number. The statements are separated by a colon.

```
140   PRINT : PRINT
```

will therefore 'print' *two* blank lines also. Lines 90 to 135 ask the user to select what is required and list the options. The last option, the program exit, has to be provided for when the user has finished his or her use of the program.

Certain versions of BASIC allow an INPUT statement to be combined with an instructional 'message' which is to be printed, eg:

```
150   INPUT "ENTER APPROPRIATE NUMBER "; A
```

will print the instruction 'Enter appropriate number' on the screen and the computer will then await the necessary input, a number from 1 to 5.

The remainder of this text will follow the above format. For those readers using a computer without this facility, two statements will be required:

    150   PRINT "ENTER APPROPRIATE NUMBER"
    155   INPUT A

It has already been stressed (p36) that the detection of invalid input and the taking of appropriate action are very important. The following condition statement will test whether a valid number (ie any number from 1 to 5) has, in fact, been entered. If not, the program switches back to line 150 and repeats the message 'Enter appropriate number'.

    157   IF A < 1 OR A > 5 THEN GOTO 150

Note the way in which relational operators (see p41) are used.

Subroutines
The program must now be directed to the appropriate subroutine which will handle the chosen function:

    160   IF A = 1 THEN GOSUB 1000
    170   IF A = 2 THEN GOSUB 2000
    180   IF A = 3 THEN GOSUB 3000
    190   IF A = 4 THEN GOSUB 4000
    200   IF A = 5 THEN GOTO 12000

A possible alternative to the several IF . . . THEN statements is, in some versions of BASIC, a single ON statement, eg:

    160   ON A GOSUB 1000, 2000, 3000, 4000

The ON statement passes control of the program to a specified line number according to the value of a numeric variable, in this instance named 'A'.

Line 200 does not direct the program to a subroutine but to the program termination point.
70

Classified sort and print out routine The first subroutine, beginning at line 1000, is for a print out of the catalogue in classified order. The data must first be sorted into a classified sequence. The sort is a bubble sort similar to the one described on p48, although this time based upon the classification number. An additional requirement, however, is that when two class numbers are transposed, the other elements relating to the particular item must also be transposed, ie C$, N$, T$ and D$ must all be repositioned so that they remain together. Here is the full subroutine:

```
1000    REM   CLASSIFIED SORT AND PRINT ROUTINE
1005    HOME
1010    FOR K = 1 TO T − 1
1020    FOR J = 1 TO T − 1
1030    IF C$(J) < C$(J+1) THEN GOTO 1160
1040    LET W$ = C$(J)
1050    LET X$ = N$(J)
1060    LET Y$ = T$(J)
1070    LET Z$ = D$(J)
1080    LET C$(J) = C$(J+1)
1090    LET N$(J) = N$(J+1)
1100    LET T$(J) = T$(J+1)
1110    LET D$(J) = D$(J+1)
1120    LET C$(J+1) = W$
1130    LET N$(J+1) = X$
1140    LET T$(J+1) = Y$
1150    LET D$(J+1) = Z$
1160    NEXT J
1170    NEXT K
1180    PRINT "CLASSIFIED LISTING"
1190    PRINT
1200    FOR I = 1 TO T
1210    PRINT C$(I);N$(I);T$(I);D$(I)
1220    NEXT I
1230    RETURN
```

The HOME, at the beginning of the subroutine, clears the screen ready to print out the listing.

The inner loop, lines 1020 to 1160, sorts on the classification number (C$) and if a transposition is necessary all the elements (C$, N$, T$ and D$) are transposed.

The outer loop, lines 1010 to 1170, governs the number of passes through the list. Note the use of the count (T) to relate the number of repetitions in the loop to the number of items in the catalogue.

Line 1180 prints the heading and lines 1200 to 1220 constitute a further loop which prints out the classified listing of the catalogue.

The last line, 1230, RETURN's the program to the main sequence. More will be said about this later.

The previously noted facility for placing more than one statement after a single line number could be useful in this section of the program to reduce the amount of detail, eg:

```
1040    LET W$ = C$(J)  :  LET X$ = N$(J)  :  LET Y$ = T$(J)
```

As indicated on p27 it may also be possible to omit the word LET, eg:

```
1040    W$ = C$(J)  :  X$ = N$(J)  :  Y$ = T$(J)
```

Whether these economies of programming can be achieved will depend upon the equipment in use.

Alphabetical sort and print out routine The subroutine for the alphabetical sort is very similar to that for the classified arrangement but the sort will be on the author's name (N$). All of the other elements must, of course, also be sorted as before.

One significant change in this routine is that the order of the elements is altered in the print out to bring the author's name to the lead position and take the class number to the end.

```
2000    REM  ALPHABETICAL SORT AND PRINT ROUTINE
2005    HOME
2010    FOR K = 1 TO T − 1
2020    FOR J = 1 TO T − 1
2030    IF N$(J) < N$(J+1) THEN GOTO 2160
2040    LET W$ = C$(J)
2050    LET X$ = N$(J)
```

```
2060   LET Y$ = T$(J)
2070   LET Z$ = D$(J)
2080   LET C$(J) = C$(J+1)
2090   LET N$(J) = N$(J+1)
2100   LET T$(J) = T$(J+1)
2110   LET D$(J) = D$(J+1)
2120   LET C$(J+1) = W$
2130   LET N$(J+1) = X$
2140   LET T$(J+1) = Y$
2150   LET D$(J+1) = Z$
2160   NEXT J
2170   NEXT K
2180   PRINT "ALPHABETICAL LISTING"
2190   PRINT
2200   FOR I = 1 TO T
2210   PRINT N$(I);T$(I);D$(I);"   ";C$(I)
2220   NEXT I
2230   RETURN
```

The differences between this routine and the classified sort and print routine occur in line 2030, where the sort is on the author's name (N$) and line 2210, where the classification number (C$) is printed last and the author's name (N$) takes the lead.

One problem not catered for in the above print routines is that of the number of entries that can be displayed on the screen at any one time which must obviously be restricted and which will be nowhere near the full one hundred items which the program can handle. The result will be that once the catalogue increases to a size beyond the screen's capacity of display, the print out will 'roll-up' the screen and only the last part of the catalogue will remain for scanning purposes. There are two possible solutions to this problem. Firstly, the print out could be transferred to a printer, where no such size restriction would apply.* Alternatively, the program could be amended so that the catalogue may be displayed section by section, so many items at a time. This latter

*The instructions for the computer configuration in use should be examined if this is required.

solution could be achieved by condition statements inserted in the printing routines at appropriate places (between lines 1210-1220 and 2210-2220) eg:

1213   IF C$(I) = C$(9) THEN INPUT "HIT RETURN TO CONTINUE ";A$

Such a statement would ensure that only the first nine items would be displayed and the remainder of the catalogue would not appear until the Return key was pressed. This 'pause' mechanism could be inserted every ten items, every twenty items, or any other number relevant to the particular v.d.u., using a 'logical operator', in this instance 'OR', eg:

1213   IF C$(I) = C$(20) OR C$(I) = C$(40) OR C$(I) = C$(60) OR C$(I) = C$(80) THEN INPUT "HIT RETURN TO CONTINUE ";A$

An alternative and more practical method would be to use a nested loop which incorporates an incremental STEP in the count. Without a STEP, which is optional, the increment is one. A loop such as:

FOR M = 1 TO 100
. . .
NEXT M

would, as we have seen, provide a means of repeating a routine one hundred times. If, however, a STEP is included then, each time round, the loop increases the initial value of the count by the STEP value, until the final value is reached. The following statements, for example:

FOR M = 3 TO 18 STEP 4
. . .
NEXT M

would enable the loop to be executed when M equals 3, 7, 11 and 15.

The statement:

FOR M = 9 TO T STEP 10

would execute the loop when M equals 9, 19, 29 and so on

up to the value T. By itself, this would simply execute the loop the appropriate number of times but the inclusion of a condition statement linking the 'M' count of this loop with the 'I' count of the print loop would provide a means of controlling the number of items to be printed at any one time, ie:

    IF C$(I) = C$(M) THEN . . .

The full additional program statements required would therefore be:

```
1213    FOR M = 9 TO T STEP 10
1215    IF C$(I) = C$(M) THEN INPUT "HIT RETURN TO
        CONTINUE ";A$ : PRINT
1217    NEXT M
```

This routine will ensure that the catalogue is printed on the screen ten items at a time (except for the beginning, when only nine items will be printed, thus leaving room for the heading 'Classified listing'). After each section of ten items has been printed, the message 'Hit Return to continue' will appear and, after the Return key has been pressed, the next ten items will be printed. The PRINT statement at the end of line 1215 is for spacing purposes.

A similar routine will be required between lines 2210 and 2220 for the alphabetical listing.

Search by class number or by author's name An ability to search data for a particular classification number, a particular author, or a particular subject etc is an obvious necessity for librarians. Such a facility is also essential for other purposes; the example that seems to occur most frequently in microcomputer systems is that of the telephone directory, when a search for a particular person and his or her telephone number is required. Whatever the application, the principle remains the same.

The subroutines beginning at lines 3000 and 4000 enable such searches to be made by this program. The IF . . . THEN statement is used to compare the character string required with those available in the data base, eg:

IF C$ = "942" THEN . . .

ie if the class number = "942" then   . . . As the computer
reads through the data it will be watching out for this condition to be satisfied.

As we shall see, the character string allocated to the
classification number is, in fact, longer than three characters
and the above statement needs revision because of this. Use
can be made of the string function LEFT$ listed on p42, eg:

IF LEFT$(C$,3) = "942" THEN . . .

ie if the first three digits on the left hand side of the classification number = "942" then . . .

The search on the author's name is very similar but this
time it is decided to search on the first four letters of the
name, eg:

IF LEFT$(N$,4) = "SMIT" THEN . . .

Here is the first subroutine in full:

```
3000    REM  SEARCH BY CLASS NUMBER
3010    HOME
3020    INPUT "ENTER CLASS NO.  - 3 FIGURE
        MAXIMUM ";A$
3030    LET C = 0
3040    HOME
3050    PRINT "RELEVANT ITEMS ARE:"
3060    PRINT
3070    FOR I = 1 TO T
3080    IF LEFT$(C$(I),3) = A$ THEN GOTO 3100
3090    GOTO 3120
3100    PRINT C$(I);N$(I);T$(I);D$(I)
3110    LET C = C + 1
3120    NEXT I
3130    IF C = 0 THEN PRINT "SORRY, NONE FOUND"
3140    RETURN
```

The subroutine first asks the user to input the string to be
searched for, which will be a three figure maximum classification number. A heading 'Relevant items are:' is printed
before a loop (lines 3070 to 3120) enabling a search to be

made through the data for the required string. The possibility that no relevant items may be found is, in this instance, catered for by a count. This is initialized in line 3030 and 'I' is added whenever details of a relevant item are printed out (lines 3100 and 3110). If, at the end of the search, the count is still equal to zero, then there are no relevant items and this is reported to the user.

The second search subroutine is very similar to the first:

```
4000    REM   SEARCH BY AUTHOR
4010    HOME
4020    PRINT "ENTER FIRST FOUR LETTERS"
4030    PRINT  :  PRINT "OF AUTHOR'S NAME"
4040    INPUT A$
4050    LET C = 0
4060    HOME
4070    PRINT "RELEVANT ITEMS ARE:"
4080    PRINT
4090    FOR I = 1 TO T
4100    IF LEFT$(N$(I),4) = A$ THEN GOTO 4120
4110    GOTO 4140
4120    PRINT N$(I);T$(I);D$(I);"   ";C$(I)
4130    LET C = C + 1
4140    NEXT I
4150    IF C = 0 THEN PRINT "SORRY, NONE FOUND"
4160    RETURN
```

The input instruction is slightly revised because of the fact that the sentence 'Enter first four letters of author's name' is over forty characters in length. It is therefore printed on two lines with a blank line between.

The above are illustrative searches. By quite simple changes in the program various search 'conditions' could be applied. We will return to this point later.

Returning to the menu
After a particular subroutine has been completed, the user cannot be left 'high and dry'; some further instruction must be supplied. In this program, the appropriate action is to offer the user the menu once again so that another (or the

77

same option) can be selected or the program can be terminated.

Each subroutine, after execution, RETURNs the program to the main sequence, line 170, 180, 190 or 200. In every instance the next instruction to be followed will be that immediately subsequent to line 200:

```
210    PRINT : INPUT "HIT M FOR MENU ";A$
220    IF A$ = "M" THEN GOTO 20
```

After the user has entered 'M' and pressed the Return key, line 220 transfers the program to line 20 to repeat the printing of the menu.

The possibility of some character other than 'M' being entered must be catered for (using <>, ie 'not equal to'):

```
230    IF A$ <> "M" THEN PRINT "YOU HAVE HIT THE
       WRONG CHARACTER"
240    PRINT
250    GOTO 210
```

Line 250 transfers the program to line 210 so that the message 'Hit M etc' will reappear.

A more economical alternative to this procedure would be to ask the user simply to 'Hit Return for Menu':

```
210    PRINT : INPUT "HIT RETURN FOR MENU ";A$
220    GOTO 20
```

However, the routine shown in lines 230 to 250 above does illustrate how a test can be made for invalid input.

The data
The number of elements of information relating to each item and the length of such elements is a matter of choice and can vary widely.

In this program, the number of elements and the length of the elements have been chosen so that the data relating to each item will fit on one 'line' of the v.d.u. screen. The screen has been assumed to be one of forty characters in width, so that all the elements must add up to this number. The 'division' selected is:

78

Classification number	6 characters
Author's name	10 characters
Title	20 characters
Date	4 characters

It is appreciated that the make-up of the data is very simple, eg author's surname only, but this is purposeful; it has been carefully calculated for ease of illustration and demonstration.

The complete set of information relating to an item is known as a *record*. Each element within the record is called a *field*.

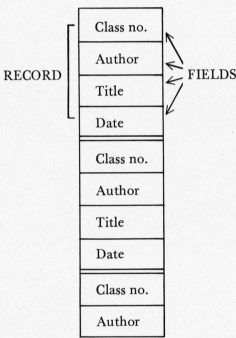

If the number of characters in a field is fixed at a maximum number, as it is in this case, then this is known as a *fixed field*. The alternative, ie no fixed number of characters, is a *variable field*.

A collection of records is referred to as a *file* and a *data base* may consist of one or more files.

If a particular fixed field is not completely filled by the

relevant class number, author, or title etc then spaces must constitute the remaining characters.

If a class number, author, or title etc is longer than a particular fixed field, then it must be truncated to the appropriate number of characters.

Here is some sample data for this program:

```
5000    DATA "636    ","SODERBURG ",
        "POPULAR PET KEEPING  ","1955"

5010    DATA "794    ","WADE        ",
        "PLAYING CHESS        ","1974"

5020    DATA "445    ","COLVER     ",
        "I CAN READ FRENCH    ","1972"

5030    DATA "942    ","FALKUS      ",
        "SPANISH ARMADA       ","1972"

5040    DATA"739    ","PORTEOUS  ",
        "COINS                ","1973"

5050    DATA "635    ","BEBB        ",
        "HANDYMAN GARDENER ","1979"

5060    DATA "799    ","PRITCHARD ",
        "LET'S GO FISHING     ","1979"

5070    DATA "797    ","COLE        ",
        "SMALL CRAFT SAFETY   ","1973"

5080    DATA "745    ","WRIGHT      ",
        "LETTERING            ","1950"
```

Classification numbers have been limited to three digits, although this is not obligatory. The other three characters in the string become spaces. A further reason for making the classification number a character string rather than a numeric variable is that we may wish to include numbers beginning with zero, eg '020', or '001'. Computers have a habit of deleting leading zeros when dealing with numbers, as indicated on p51, and the use of a character string will prevent this.

Any number of items up to a maximum of one hundred could be placed in data statements. Having left plenty of space, in terms of line numbers, for this data, a further "rogue" data statement is included:

```
10000    DATA "END    ","            ",
         "            ","      "
```

Coupled with line 14:

```
14    IF C$(I) = "END       " THEN GOTO 10000
```

this provides an "escape" from the READ loop as previously explained.

The next to last line of the program (12000) prints the message 'Goodbye' before the program is terminated. The user would receive this message after selecting option '5' of the menu, 'Exit this program'.

```
12000    PRINT : PRINT : PRINT "GOODBYE"
12010    END
```

Program listing
Here is a listing of the full program in sequence:

```
  5    REM  CATALOGUING SIMULATION
  7    LET T = 0
 10    DIM C$(100),N$(100),T$(100),D$(100)
 11    FOR I = 1 TO 100
 12    READ C$(I),N$(I),T$(I),D$(I)
 14    IF C$(I) = "END      " THEN GOTO 20
 16    LET T = T + 1
 18    NEXT I
 20    HOME
 30    PRINT TAB(9) "CATALOGUING SIMULATION"
 40    PRINT
 50    FOR A= 1 TO 40
 60    PRINT "*";
 70    NEXT A
 80    PRINT : PRINT
 90    PRINT "DO YOU REQUIRE:"
100    PRINT : PRINT TAB (8) "1  CLASSIFIED PRINT OUT"
110    PRINT TAB(8) "2  ALPHABETICAL PRINT OUT"
120    PRINT TAB(8) "3  SEARCH BY CLASS NO"
130    PRINT TAB(8) "4  SEARCH BY AUTHOR"
135    PRINT TAB(8) "5  EXIT THIS PROGRAM"
140    PRINT : PRINT
```

81

```
150     INPUT "ENTER APPROPRIATE NUMBER "; A
157     IF A < 1 OR A > 5 THEN GOTO 150
160     IF A = 1 THEN GOSUB 1000
170     IF A = 2 THEN GOSUB 2000
180     IF A = 3 THEN GOSUB 3000
190     IF A = 4 THEN GOSUB 4000
200     IF A = 5 THEN GOTO 12000
210     PRINT : INPUT "HIT M FOR MENU ";A$
220     IF A$ = "M" THEN GOTO 20
230     IF A$ <> "M" THEN PRINT "YOU HAVE HIT THE
        WRONG CHARACTER"
240     PRINT
250     GOTO 210
1000    REM   CLASSIFIED SORT AND PRINT ROUTINE
1005    HOME
1010    FOR K = 1 TO T − 1
1020    FOR J = 1 TO T − 1
1030    IF C$(J)<C$(J+1) THEN GOTO 1160
1040    LET W$ = C$(J)
1050    LET X$ = N$(J)
1060    LET Y$ = T$(J)
1070    LET Z$ = D$(J)
1080    LET C$(J) = C$(J+1)
1090    LET N$(J) = N$(J+1)
1100    LET T$(J) = T$(J+1)
1110    LET D$(J) = D$(J+1)
1120    LET C$(J+1) = W$
1130    LET N$(J+1) = X$
1140    LET T$(J+1) = Y$
1150    LET D$(J+1) = Z$
1160    NEXT J
1170    NEXT K
1180    PRINT "CLASSIFIED LISTING"
1190    PRINT
1200    FOR I = 1 TO T
1210    PRINT C$(I);N$(I);T$(I);D$(I)
1213    FOR M = 9 TO T STEP 10
1215    IF C$(I) = C$(M) THEN INPUT "HIT RETURN TO
        CONTINUE ";A$ : PRINT
1217    NEXT M
```

```
1220    NEXT I
1230    RETURN
2000    REM   ALPHABETICAL SORT AND PRINT ROUTINE
2005    HOME
2010    FOR K = 1 TO T − 1
2020    FOR J = 1 TO T − 1
2030    IF N$(J) < N$(J+1) THEN GOTO 2160
2040    LET W$ = C$(J)
2050    LET X$ = N$(J)
2060    LET Y$ = T$(J)
2070    LET Z$ = D$(J)
2080    LET C$(J) = C$(J+1)
2090    LET N$(J) = N$(J+1)
2100    LET T$(J) = T$(J+1)
2110    LET D$(J) = D$(J+1)
2120    LET C$(J+1) = W$
2130    LET N$(J+1) = X$
2140    LET T$(J+1) = Y$
2150    LET D$(J+1) = Z$
2160    NEXT J
2170    NEXT K
2180    PRINT "ALPHABETICAL LISTING"
2190    PRINT
2200    FOR I = 1 TO T
2210    PRINT N$(I);T$(I);D$(I);"   ";C$(I)
2213    FOR M = 9 TO T STEP 10
2215    IF N$(I) = N$(M) THEN INPUT "HIT RETURN TO
        CONTINUE ";A$ : PRINT
2217    NEXT M
2220    NEXT I
2230    RETURN
3000    REM   SEARCH BY CLASS NUMBER
3010    HOME
3020    INPUT "ENTER CLASS NO. − 3 FIGURE MAXIMUM
        ";A$
3030    LET C = 0
3040    HOME
3050    PRINT "RELEVANT ITEMS ARE:"
3060    PRINT
3070    FOR I = 1 TO T
```

```
3080    IF LEFT$(C$(I),3) = A$ THEN GOTO 3100
3090    GOTO 3120
3100    PRINT C$(I);N$(I);T$(I);D$(I)
3110    LET C = C + 1
3120    NEXT I
3130    IF C = 0 THEN PRINT "SORRY, NONE FOUND"
3140    RETURN
4000    REM   SEARCH BY AUTHOR
4010    HOME
4020    PRINT "ENTER FIRST FOUR LETTERS"
4030    PRINT : PRINT "OF AUTHOR'S NAME" : PRINT
4040    INPUT A$
4050    LET C = 0
4060    HOME
4070    PRINT "RELEVANT ITEMS ARE:"
4080    PRINT
4090    FOR I = 1 TO T
4100    IF LEFT$(N$(I),4) = A$ THEN GOTO 4120
4110    GOTO 4140
4120    PRINT N$(I);T$(I);D$(I);"   ";C$(I)
4130    LET C = C + 1
4140    NEXT I
4150    IF C = 0 THEN PRINT "SORRY, NONE FOUND"
4160    RETURN
5000    DATA "636     ","SODERBURG ",
        "POPULAR PET KEEPING   ","1955"
5010    DATA "794     ","WADE         ",
        "PLAYING CHESS          ","1974"
5020    DATA "445     ","COLVER      ",
        "I CAN READ FRENCH      ","1972"
5030    DATA "942     ","FALKUS      ",
        "SPANISH ARMADA         ","1972"
5040    DATA "739     ","PORTEOUS   ",
        "COINS                  ","1973"
5050    DATA "635     ","BEBB         ",
        "HANDYMAN GARDENER ","1979"
5060    DATA "799     ","PRITCHARD  ",
        "LET'S GO FISHING        ","1979"
5070    DATA ,,797     ","COLE        ",
        "SMALL CRAFT SAFETY    ","1973"
```

```
5080    DATA "745      ","WRIGHT       ",
        "LETTERING                ","1950"
10000   DATA "END    ","              ",
        "                        ","      "
12000   PRINT : PRINT : PRINT "GOODBYE"
12010   END
```

The program in operation
When a user operates the program, using the command:

    RUN

the following menu will appear on the screen:

```
+-------------------------------------------------+
|                                                 |
|            CATALOGUING SIMULATION               |
|                                                 |
|    ***************************************       |
|                                                 |
|                                                 |
|    DO YOU REQUIRE:                              |
|                                                 |
|            1   CLASSIFIED PRINT OUT              |
|            2   ALPHABETICAL PRINT OUT            |
|            3   SEARCH BY CLASS NO                |
|            4   SEARCH BY AUTHOR                  |
|            5   EXIT THIS PROGRAM                 |
|                                                 |
|    ENTER APPROPRIATE NUMBER                      |
|                                                 |
+-------------------------------------------------+
```

If option '1' is selected, then, after a brief pause whilst
the data is sorted into the relevant sequence (the pause will
get longer as the number of items to be sorted increases!), a
'Classified listing' will appear:

```
CLASSIFIED LISTING

445  COLVER       I CAN READ FRENCH      1972
635  BEBB         HANDYMAN GARDENER      1979
636  SODERBERG    POPULAR PET KEEPING    1955
739  PORTEOUS     COINS                  1973
745  WRIGHT       LETTERING              1950
794  WADE         PLAYING CHESS          1974
797  COLE         SMALL CRAFT SAFETY     1973
799  PRITCHARD    LET'S GO FISHING       1979
942  FALKUS       SPANISH ARMADA         1972


HIT RETURN TO CONTINUE
```

Pressing the Return key will cause the next section of the catalogue to appear and when the print out, screen by screen, of the catalogue is complete, the message:

HIT M FOR MENU

will be seen. After the user has followed this instruction and pressed the Return key, the menu will reappear immediately:

```
             CATALOGUING SIMULATION

******************************************

     DO YOU REQUIRE:

             1   CLASSIFIED PRINT OUT
             2   ALPHABETICAL PRINT OUT
             3   SEARCH BY CLASS NO
             4   SEARCH BY AUTHOR
             5   EXIT THIS PROGRAM

     ENTER APPROPRIATE NUMBER
```

If option '2' is now selected, an 'Alphabetical listing' will appear, again after a brief pause for the sort and again section by section:

```
ALPHABETICAL LISTING

BEBB         HANDYMAN GARDENER 1979   635
COLE         SMALL CRAFT SAFETY  1973   797
COLVER       I CAN READ FRENCH   1972   445
FALKUS       SPANISH ARMADA      1972   942
PORTEOUS     COINS               1973   739
PRITCHARD    LET'S GO FISHING    1979   799
SODERBERG    POPULAR PET KEEPING 1955   636
WADE         PLAYING CHESS       1974   794
WRIGHT       LETTERING           1950   745

HIT RETURN TO CONTINUE
```

A return to the menu and the selection of option '3' will cause the following instruction to appear:

```
ENTER CLASS NO. — 3 FIGURE MAXIMUM
```

Suppose that

```
445
```

is entered; the computer will respond with:

```
RELEVANT ITEMS ARE:
445  COLVER      I CAN READ FRENCH      1972
HIT M FOR MENU
```

If a particular classification number searched for, eg:

```
136
```

is not represented in the data base, the computer will deliver the message:

```
RELEVANT ITEMS ARE:
SORRY, NONE FOUND
HIT M FOR MENU
```

A similar process is followed for a search on an author's name but the order of the elements in the print out will change, eg:

```
ENTER FIRST FOUR LETTERS
OF AUTHOR'S NAME

SODE
```

```
RELEVANT ITEMS ARE:
SODERBURG POPULAR PET KEEPING 1955   636
HIT M FOR MENU
```

The menu can continue to be used in this way until the user has obtained all of the information that is required. Option '5' will then be selected and the message:

```
GOODBYE
```

will appear on the screen.

Note that although only nine items were placed in the data base in this instance, further items can be inserted at any time simply by adding more data statements, eg:

```
5090   DATA "610     ","JOHNSON     ","MEDICAL
       SYMPTOMS    ","1976"
```

Items can be deleted or withdrawn simply by entering the appropriate line number and pressing the Return key:

```
5090
```

Further modification of the program

It has been assumed, throughout this program, that the user would have been aware that the Return key has to be pressed after each piece of input. Appropriate instructions could, of course, have been printed on to the screen each time that this was required.

There is always more than one way of writing a program in order to achieve a desired result and it is not claimed that the above example is either the best or the only solution to the problem.

In addition, there is always room for improvement in a program. This one would require modification, for instance, in order to sort on more than one level. If, for example, two class numbers were the same, a further sort would be required within that class number to alphabetize the authors' names. If authors' names were the same, a sort would be required on titles. Further modifications could include instructions for entering data, or a means of switching the output to a printer so that a hard copy could be obtained when necessary.

Additional tests for invalid input could also be built in. Such tests could be made, for instance, in order to ensure that the correct number of characters has been entered when a user is searching on class number or author. The LEN(A$) function (see p42) could be utilized for this purpose, eg:

IF LEN(A$) < > 4 THEN . . .

The search subroutines in fact comprise an area where there is considerable scope for change. There is no need to limit searching to the first four letters of an author's name* or the first three digits of a classification number. Various search conditions could be allowed for and searches could be made on any element of a record deemed necessary, eg the date of publication. The reader should now be able to formulate other possible search strategies using the statements of BASIC and the string functions.

It is possible to combine conditions by using logical operators. An example of the use of the 'OR' operator has already been given (see p74). 'AND' is another logical operator

*A method of searching on the full author's name will be explained at a later point in this text.

which can be utilized in searches. For example, if it is required to search on an author's surname and forename, a variable name could be allocated to each, eg A$ = surname and B$ = forename. A statement such as:

IF A$ = "SMITH" AND B$ = "JOHN" THEN . . .

would enable such a search to be made.

On the previous page (and on p78) the relational expression <>, meaning 'not equal to', ie 'less than' or 'greater than', was used. This expression could improve the program if inserted in place of the equals sign in lines 3080 and 4100. Lies 3090 and 4110 would then be superfluous thus avoiding, in each instance, two consecutive GOTOs, eg:

```
3080    IF LEFT$(C$(I),3) <> A$ THEN GOTO 3120
3100    PRINT C$(I);N$(I);T$(I);D$(I)
```

The second illustrative program is concerned with the simulation of an issue system for a library service point.

The major requirements for such a system are that each copy of an item in the stock of the library is allocated a unique number and that each reader who uses the library is also allocated a unique number. An 'issue' can then be recorded by matching an item number with a reader number.

Numbers can be 'meaningful', that is they can represent, in digit form, particular information. In this way, 'counts' can produce a variety of library statistics apart from the total issue.

It may be necessary to introduce other features into the system: for example, it is very useful to be able to make the computer indicate that an item is a 'reservation', that is that it is required by a particular reader; it can be 'trapped' and kept to one side for that person.

The first part of the program might enable a title frame to be printed, which could include the name of the library:

```
5    REM  ISSUE SYSTEM SIMULATION
10   HOME
20   PRINT TAB(16) "X  LIBRARY"
30   PRINT : PRINT TAB(15) "ISSUE SYSTEM"
40   PRINT : PRINT : PRINT : PRINT
50   INPUT "PRESS THE RETURN KEY TO CONTINUE";F$
```

Next, an array of character strings to contain item number and reader number must be established. Despite being 'numbers', character strings are used for this data because of the need to 'search' strings for particular features:

```
100    DIM B$(100),R$(100)
```

The (100) is an arbitrary number; it will depend on the number of issues likely to be made during a certain cycle. B$ relates to the variable book, or item, number and R$ relates to the reader number.

91

The following loop will enable item and reader numbers to be input:

```
120   FOR J = 1 TO 100
210   INPUT "ENTER BOOK NUMBER  ";B$(J)
220   INPUT "ENTER READER NUMBER ";R$(J)
330   NEXT J
```

Instructions can be printed on to the screen to inform the user how to record an issue:

```
130   HOME
140   PRINT "TO RECORD AN ISSUE ENTER BOOK NO."
150   PRINT "FOLLOWED BY READER NO."
```

The total issue may be less than one hundred and a loop 'escape' route must therefore be provided:

```
180   PRINT "WHEN ISSUE CYCLE IS FINISHED"
190   PRINT "ENTER END AS BOOK NO. AND"  :  PRINT
      "PRESS RETURN FOR READER NO."

320   IF B$(J) = "END" THEN . . .
```

As previously indicated, it will obviously be useful to obtain a 'count' of the total issue and this is quite easily achieved. A count 'T' is initialized outside the input loop:

```
110   LET T = 0
```

and every time an issue is recorded, '1' is added to the total:

```
210   INPUT "ENTER BOOK NUMBER  ";B$(J)
220   INPUT "ENTER READER NUMBER  ";R$(J)
230   LET T = T + 1
```

The total issue at the end of a cycle can now be found by printing out 'T'.

But what if other 'counts' are required, eg total fiction issue, total non-fiction issue, or the total issue of any other

92

specified type of material? This is where 'meaningful' numbers can play their part. Suppose that we stipulate that every fiction book number must begin with a '1' and every non-fiction book number with a '2'. A count 'F' can be used to total the fiction issue and a count 'NF' to total the non-fiction issue. These must first be initialized:

```
110    LET F = 0: LET NF = 0
```

Every time an appropriate issue is made, '1' can be added to the relevant total:

```
240    IF LEFT$(B$(J),1) = "1" THEN LET F = F + 1
250    IF LEFT$(B$(J),1) = "2" THEN LET NF = NF + 1
```

We could go further; as an example 'music' could be indicated by a '1' as the second digit following the '2' for non-fiction, ie '21'. A count 'M' could be used to total the music issue:

```
110    LET M = 0
```

```
260    IF LEFT$(B$(J),2) = "21" THEN LET M = M + 1
```

In this way, a whole variety of statistical information may be obtained by designing the numbers around required data. The reader number could be similarly treated, if so desired, to indicate, for example, male readers, female readers, juvenile readers, non-resident readers etc.

Here is that section of the program which prints out the statistical information automatically whenever an issue cycle is terminated:

```
350    PRINT "TOTAL ISSUE = ";T − 1
360    PRINT "TOTAL FICTION ISSUE = ";F
370    PRINT "TOTAL NON−FICTION ISSUE = ";NF
380    PRINT "TOTAL MUSIC ISSUE = ";M
```

Note that '1' is deducted from the count T to allow for the 'END' input as book number when finishing the issue cycle.

It may well be that, for the purposes of checking etc a 'print out' of the actual issue, ie the book and reader numbers, would be required:

93

```
390    PRINT "DO YOU REQUIRE PRINT-OUT OF ISSUE? "
400    INPUT "Y/N ";A$
410    IF A$ = "N" THEN . . .
420    IF A$ = "Y" THEN HOME
430    PRINT "ISSUE LISTING"
440    PRINT "BOOK NO.","READER NO."
450    PRINT
460    FOR J = 1 TO 100
470    PRINT B$(J),R$(J)
480    IF B$(J) = "END" THEN . . .
490    NEXT J
```

A check for invalid input should be included:

```
425    IF A$ < "N" OR A$ > "N" AND A$ < "Y" OR A$ > "Y"
       THEN GOTO 400
```

This check will ensure that if anything other than 'Y' or 'N' is entered the program will return to line 400 and the 'Y/N' prompt will be repeated.

Note the use not only of relational operators (see p41) but also of the logical operators 'AND' and 'OR', which enable quite complex conditional statements to be formulated.

What if 'Miss Jones' suddenly appears at the issue desk with a list of book numbers which need to be 'reserved'? Can these numbers be input to the computer and the program designed so that the computer responds in some way when one of the required numbers is being processed?

The issue cycle could be interrupted to allow the numbers that need to be 'stopped' to be entered:

```
160    PRINT "IF RESERVATION IS REQUIRED"
170    PRINT "ENTER RES AS BOOK NO. AND" :
       PRINT "PRESS RETURN FOR READER NO."

270    IF B$(J) = "RES" THEN GOSUB 1000

1000   HOME
1010   LET T = T − 1
1020   PRINT "ENTER NOS. OF BOOKS TO BE RESERVED"
1030   PRINT "TYPE DONE WHEN FINISHED"
1040   FOR I = D TO 100
```

```
1050    INPUT X$(I)
1060    LET C = C + 1 : LET D = D + 1
1070    IF X$(I) = "DONE" THEN RETURN
1080    NEXT I
```

It should now be reasonably easy for the reader to understand how this part of the program operates. Note that any
number of reservation numbers up to a hundred may be
input. Note also that, as we do not wish to count the input
'RES' as an issue, '1' is deducted from the count to keep it
correct. There are one or two other features which need a
further word of explanation. There is, as yet, no array for
the string variable X$. This would have to be included in the
DIM statement:

```
100     DIM B$(100),R$(100),X$(100)
```

The statement FOR I = D TO 100 may be puzzling. The
count 'D' relates to the number of reservations made. It may
well be necessary to interrupt the issue cycle more than once
to enter reservations. 'D' will progressively increase and thus
ensure that no more one hundred reservations can be made in
total, which would conflict with the DIM statement array.
The count 'C' is used in a nested loop to compare issue
numbers with reservation numbers:

```
280     FOR I = 1 TO C
290     IF B$(J) = X$(I) THEN INPUT "RESERVATION
        PRESS RETURN TO CONTINUE";G$
310     NEXT I
```

This loop will cause all issue numbers to be compared with all
reservation numbers and when a 'match' is found the computer
prints 'RESERVATION'. On some computers a FLASH, or
some such command, is available which causes the print out
to 'flash' alternately from black on white to white on black.
This would be a useful feature in this instance as it would make
the 'RESERVATION' warning more noticeable:

```
280     FOR I = 1 TO C
290     FLASH : IF B$(J) = D$(I) THEN INPUT
        "RESERVATION PRESS RETURN TO CONTINUE";G$
```

95

```
300    NORMAL
310    NEXT I
```

The warning would continue to flash until the Return key is pressed. The NORMAL command in line 300 returns the program to a non-flashing display.

The counts 'C' and 'D' have yet to be initialized:

```
110    LET C = 0 : LET D = 1
```

'D' is initialized at '1', so that line 1040 will begin the reservation loop at '1'.

When an issue cycle is completed and the issue totals have been output, the program has finished and a farewell message can be printed:

```
5000    PRINT "ISSUE CYCLE IS NOW COMPLETE"
5010    PRINT "GOODBYE"
```

Program listing

Here is the complete listing of the program. To improve the layout of information printed on the screen, a number of blank lines have been inserted where necessary using the PRINT statement:

```
  5    REM   ISSUE SYSTEM SIMULATION
 10    HOME
 20    PRINT TAB(16) "X    LIBRARY"
 30    PRINT : PRINT TAB(15) "ISSUE SYSTEM"
 40    PRINT : PRINT : PRINT : PRINT
 50    INPUT "PRESS THE RETURN KEY TO CONTINUE";F$
100    DIM B$(100),R$(100),X$(100)
110    LET T = 0 : F = 0 : NF = 0 : M = 0 : C = 0 : D = 1
120    FOR J = 1 TO 100
130    HOME
140    PRINT "TO RECORD AN ISSUE ENTER BOOK NO."
150    PRINT "FOLLOWED BY READER NO."
160    PRINT : PRINT : PRINT "IF RESERVATION IS
       REQUIRED"
170    PRINT "ENTER RES AS BOOK NO. AND" : PRINT
       "PRESS RETURN FOR READER NO."
```

```
180    PRINT : PRINT : PRINT "WHEN ISSUE CYCLE IS
       FINISHED"
190    PRINT "ENTER END AS BOOK NO. AND" : PRINT
       "PRESS RETURN FOR READER NO."
200    PRINT : PRINT
210    INPUT "ENTER BOOK NUMBER  ";B$(J)
220    INPUT "ENTER READER NUMBER  ";R$(J)
230    LET T = T + 1
240    IF LEFT$(B$(J),1) = "1" THEN LET F = F + 1
250    IF LEFT$(B$(J),1) = "2" THEN LET NF = NF + 1
260    IF LEFT$(B$(J),2) = "21" THEN LET M = M + 1
270    IF B$(J) = "RES" THEN GOSUB 1000
280    FOR I = 1 TO C
290    FLASH : PRINT : IF B$(J) = X$(J) THEN INPUT
       "RESERVATION   PRESS RETURN TO CONTINUE";G$
300    NORMAL
310    NEXT I
320    IF B$(J) = "END" THEN GOTO 340
330    NEXT J
340    HOME
350    PRINT "TOTAL ISSUE = ";T - 1
360    PRINT "TOTAL FICTION ISSUE = ";F
370    PRINT "TOTAL NON-FICTION ISSUE = ";NF
380    PRINT "TOTAL MUSIC ISSUE = ";M
390    PRINT : PRINT "DO YOU REQUIRE PRINT-OUT OF
       ISSUE? "
400    INPUT "Y/N ";A$
410    IF A$ = "N" THEN GOTO 5000
420    IF A$ = "Y" THEN HOME
425    IF A$ < "N" OR A$ > "N" AND A$ < "Y" OR A$ > "Y"
       THEN GOTO 400
430    PRINT "ISSUE LISTING"
440    PRINT : PRINT "BOOK NO.","READER NO."
450    PRINT
460    FOR J = 1 TO 100
470    PRINT B$(J),R$(J)
480    IF B$(J) = "END" THEN GOTO 5000
490    NEXT J
1000   HOME
1010   LET T = T - 1
```

```
1020    PRINT "ENTER NOS. OF BOOKS TO BE RESERVED"
1030    PRINT : PRINT "TYPE DONE WHEN FINISHED" : PRINT
1040    FOR I = D TO 100
1050    INPUT X$(I)
1060    LET C = C + 1  :  D = D + 1
1070    IF X$(I) = "DONE" THEN RETURN
1080    NEXT I
5000    PRINT  : PRINT  : PRINT "ISSUE CYCLE IS NOW
        COMPLETE"
5010    PRINT  : PRINT "GOODBYE"
```

The program in operation
When the command

    RUN

is input to operate the program, the following will appear on
the screen:

```
+-------------------------------------------+
|                                           |
|               X  LIBRARY                  |
|                                           |
|              ISSUE SYSTEM                 |
|                                           |
|                                           |
|     PRESS THE RETURN KEY TO CONTINUE      |
|                                           |
+-------------------------------------------+
```

After the Return key is pressed, the above will disappear and
in its place the user will see:

```
+-------------------------------------------+
|                                           |
|   TO RECORD AN ISSUE ENTER BOOK NO.       |
|   FOLLOWED BY READER NO.                  |
|                                           |
|   IF RESERVATION IS REQUIRED              |
|   ENTER RES AS BOOK NO. AND               |
|   PRESS RETURN FOR READER NO.             |
|                                           |
|   WHEN ISSUE CYCLE IS FINISHED            |
|   ENTER END AS BOOK NO. AND               |
|   PRESS RETURN FOR READER NO.             |
|                                           |
|   ENTER BOOK NUMBER                       |
|                                           |
+-------------------------------------------+
```

When the book number is entered, the computer will request the reader number:

> ENTER READER NUMBER

After the reader number is entered, the screen again displays the instructions for recording an issue and awaits the next pair of numbers.

If a five digit number is used for each book, the first two digits will be used to indicate fiction, non-fiction etc and the remaining three digits can be used as a unique accession number identifier. This would allow for up to 1,000 items (000 to 999). A three digit reader number would allow for 1,000 readers.

These numbers will have been allocated as the books were added to stock or as the readers registered.

Suppose that the first ten issues consisted of the following numbers:

ENTER BOOK NUMBER	ENTER READER NUMBER
10123	523
10456	167
20532	432
21370	235
20187	462
20258	136
10523	137
10365	472
10293	135
20174	341

'Miss Jones' then arrives with the number of a book to be reserved. Instead of the next issue, 'RES' is entered as the book number and, instead of a reader number the user simply presses the Return key. (This means, of course, that the Return key has to be pressed twice, for the pressing of the Return key is the normal way of signalling to the computer that the user has completed any necessary input and that the computer should continue with the next step of its instructions.) On the screen will now appear:

```
ENTER NOS. OF BOOKS TO BE RESERVED

TYPE DONE WHEN FINISHED
```

The number required can now be input, suppose that it is:

```
20361
```

This is the only number to be reserved, so

```
DONE
```

can now be entered and the program will then return to the main program sequence and display again the instructions for recording an issue:

```
ENTER BOOK NUMBER  21465  ENTER READER NUMBER  415
                   20634                        264
                   10357                        352
                   20361                        414
```

At this point the screen will print:

```
RESERVATION   PRESS RETURN TO CONTINUE
```

as the book being issued corresponds with the reservation number. 'RESERVATION' will continue to 'flash' until the Return key is pressed, this pause giving the operator time to 'stop' the book.

The issue cycle can now continue:

```
ENTER BOOK NUMBER  20391  ENTER READER NUMBER  147
                   20867                        471
                   20425                        452
```

At this point, it is time for the library to close for the day and the operator therefore enters 'END', as instructed. The computer now displays a summary of the issue figures:

100

```
TOTAL ISSUE = 17
TOTAL FICTION ISSUE = 6
TOTAL NON-FICTION ISSUE = 11
TOTAL MUSIC ISSUE = 2

DO YOU REQUIRE PRINT-OUT OF ISSUE?
Y/N
```

If 'Y' is entered, then an issue listing is provided:

```
ISSUE LISTING

BOOK NO.              READER NO.

10123                523
10456                167
20532                432
21370                235
20187                462
20258                136
10523                137
10365                472
10293                135
20174                341
RES
21465                415
20634                264
10357                352
20361                414
20391                147
20867                471
20425                452

END

ISSUE CYCLE IS NOW COMPLETE

GOODBYE
```

If a print-out of the issue was not required and 'N' was entered, only the 'Goodbye' message would be printed.

Further modification of the program
The trained librarian and, indeed, any other keen minded reader, will appreciate that the program, as so described, falls short of what would be necessary to operate a complete circulation system. Such a system would not only require an issue cycle but also a *return* cycle. The reservation routine would obviously be better placed in the latter, as it would be more appropriate to 'trap' an item when it is being returned rather than when it is issued.

The two lists, an 'issue' list of book and reader numbers and a 'return' list of book and reader numbers would have to be periodically compared, so that returned items could be deleted from issued lists. After a set period of issue, the latter lists would be examined, by the computer, and the details of any outstanding issues noted as 'overdue'. The computer could be programmed to print the necessary over-due notices automatically but, in order to do this, a reader file would have to be referred to so that reader numbers could be translated into names and addresses. If it were considered necessary to print book details, as well as book numbers, on the overdue notices, a 'stock' file would also have to be consulted. Such 'data bases' could follow the 'cataloguing' principles explained earlier in this text. Even if not needed for overdue notices, these files would obviously be required for other purposes.

It can be seen that the system is now becoming rather complex; it would require multiple data bases and multiple programs. A full explanation is outside the scope of this book as it would involve file handling (see Appendix One).

Two further points relating to the program need to be stressed. Firstly, it would be unnecessary, and indeed a little tedious, to keep repeating the instructions for every issue once the operator is aware of what is required. Secondly, the book numbers and readers' numbers need not necessarily be entered via a keyboard. They could more usefully be input, for example, by means of a 'light pen' which could 'read' bar-code labels on books and readers' tickets.

Figure 3 'Reading' the number from a bar-coded label on a reader's ticket by means of a light pen.

The last illustrative program is short in length but important in nature for it demonstrates how a series of character strings may be searched to see if any of them contain certain specified characters, searching for a string within a string, as it were.

The first part of the program sets up a list in the usual way. Again, the nominal figure of one hundred is selected for the number of items in the list. Each item consists of one character string:

```
10   REM  SEARCHING THROUGH A STRING
20   DIM A$(100)
```

The items, in this instance, are document titles. For ease of explanation, each of these title strings is 'fixed' at thirty characters. If a title is less than thirty characters, then the remaining characters are input as spaces. Any title more than thirty characters in length would have to be truncated. Here are ten examples of relevant data statements:

```
200   DATA "HISTORY OF ENGLAND            "
210   DATA "HOME NURSING                  "
220   DATA "COSTUME THROUGH THE AGES      "
230   DATA "BETTER PHOTOGRAPHY            "
240   DATA "BOOK OF HOME COOKERY          "
250   DATA "WHICH WORD PROCESSOR          "
260   DATA "HORSES AND RIDERS             "
270   DATA "INTRODUCTION TO ALGEBRA       "
280   DATA "HEATING AND VENTILATION       "
290   DATA "PORCELAIN MARKS OF THE WORLD  "
```

This list would be 'read' using a FOR . . . NEXT loop and the now familiar count and 'escape' route are provided:

```
30   LET C = 0
40   FOR I = 1 TO 100
50   READ A$(I)
60   IF A$(I) = "999              " THEN
     GOTO . . .
```

```
70    LET C = C + 1
80    NEXT I
```

. . .

```
1400   DATA "999                        "
```

The required search term is entered following a 'prompt' message and, as a count of the number of characters in the search term is needed, this is done using the LEN character string function (see p42).

```
90    HOME
100   PRINT "ENTER SEARCH TERM"
110   INPUT B$
120   LET L = LEN(B$)
```

The data statements are searched using a nested loop and the MID$ string function enables the search term to be compared with different sections of each string:

```
130   REM  SEARCHING THE STRING
140   FOR I = 1 TO C
150   FOR J = 1 TO 30
160   IF MID$(A$(I),J,L) = B$ THEN PRINT A$(I)
170   NEXT J
180   NEXT I
```

The outer loop, lines 140 to 180, works through the list, looking successively at each of the title strings. The inner loop, lines 150 to 170, searches through each individual string. The 'FOR J = 1 TO 30' loop is used to progress through the string from the first letter to the last. As this progression continues, the search term B$ is compared with specific parts of the title string. Let us examine in a little more detail how this is done.

In the 'MID$(A$(I),J,L)' statement, 'J' progresses from 1 to 30 and L is the number of characters in the search term. If the search term is 'Algebra', for example, then L would equal 7 and

MID$(A$(I),J,L) would equal MID$(A$(I),1,7)
then it would equal MID$(A$(I),2,7) and so on.

105

The effect of this is to move 'Algebra' through each string comparing it with each series of seven characters, ie:

INTRODUCTION TO ALGEBRA
ALGEBRA
 ALGEBRA
  ALGEBRA

until, when J = 17, a 'match' is found:

INTRODUCTION TO ALGEBRA
ALGEBRA

It is clear that there is no need to search the string the full thirty times. The maximum number of comparisons that could be required is, in fact, (30—L) + 1. Take, for example, a title which is a full thirty characters in length, eg:

HOLIDAY GUIDE TO GREAT BRITAIN

If a search is made for 'BRITAIN', a match will be found at the 24th comparison, ie (30—L) + 1 = (30—7) + 1 = 24. Line 150, therefore, should, more accurately, read:

```
150    FOR I = 1 TO 30—L+1
```

The last part of the program is a simple routine which gives the user the option of searching again under another term, or of exiting the program:

```
1500    PRINT "DO YOU WISH TO SEARCH AGAIN? "
1510    INPUT "Y/N ";C$
1520    IF C$ = "Y" THEN GOTO 90
1530    PRINT "GOODBYE"
1540    END
```

Note the way in which the final lines of the program are formulated so that an 'IF C$ = "N"' decision is not required. Any input other than 'Y' will result in the 'Goodbye' message.

Program listing
Here is a listing of the full program in sequence with one or two additional PRINT statements added for spacing purposes:
106

```
10    REM  SEARCHING THROUGH A STRING
20    DIM A$(100)
30    LET C = 0
40    FOR I = 1 TO 100
50    READ A$(I)
60    IF A$(I) = "999              " THEN
      GOTO 90
70    LET C = C + 1
80    NEXT I
90    HOME
100   PRINT "ENTER SEARCH TERM"
105   PRINT : PRINT
110   INPUT B$
115   PRINT : PRINT
120   LET L = LEN(B$)
130   REM  SEARCHING THE STRING
140   FOR I = 1 TO C
150   FOR J = 1 TO 30-L+1
160   IF MID$(A$(I),J,L) = B$ THEN PRINT A$(I)
170   NEXT J
180   NEXT I
200   DATA "HISTORY OF ENGLAND            "
210   DATA "HOME NURSING                  "
220   DATA "COSTUME THROUGH THE AGES      "
230   DATA "BETTER PHOTOGRAPHY            "
240   DATA "BOOK OF HOME COOKERY          "
250   DATA "WHICH WORD PROCESSOR          "
260   DATA "HORSES AND RIDERS             "
270   DATA "INTRODUCTION TO ALGEBRA       "
280   DATA "HEATING AND VENTILATION       "
290   DATA "PORCELAIN MARKS OF THE WORLD  "
1400  DATA "999                           "
1500  PRINT : PRINT : PRINT "DO YOU WISH TO SEARCH
      AGAIN? "
1510  INPUT "Y/N  ";C$
1520  IF C$ = "Y" THEN GOTO 90
1530  PRINT : PRINT "GOODBYE"
1540  END
```

The program in operation
When the program is RUN, the instruction

> ENTER SEARCH TERM
> ?

will appear on the screen.
   Suppose that

> HISTORY

is entered, then the computer will respond with

> HISTORY OF ENGLAND
>
> DO YOU WISH TO SEARCH AGAIN?
> Y/N

If "Y" is entered, then

> ENTER SEARCH TERM
> ?

will reappear. If

> ENGLAND

is then entered, the computer will again respond with

> HISTORY OF ENGLAND

   If the search term

> HOME

were entered, the computer would list the two relevant titles in the data base

> HOME NURSING
> BOOK OF HOME COOKERY

108

It can be seen that the computer will search for any length of term from a single character to a full title. A search for HOME or COOK or COOKERY or HOME COOKERY would still produce

| BOOK OF HOME COOKERY |

Further modification of the program
The ability to search through character strings is extremely useful. Not only titles but other strings such as abstracts of documents or articles, for example, could be searched.

One facility which is not included in the program is a routine for indicating that no relevant items have been found, when this is the result of a search. Such a modification could be made in a similar manner to that indicated in the cataloguing simulation on p77.

Conversely, this program suggests a way in which the earlier cataloguing simulation could be improved. The LEN function could be used to enable a search on the full author's name to be made.

Modifying the cataloguing simulation program to enable a search to be made on the full author's surname
Here are the alterations to the program which would be necessary to enable a search on the full author's name to be made:

```
4020    PRINT "ENTER AUTHOR'S NAME"
4045    LET L = LEN(A$)
4100    IF LEFT$(N$(I),L) = A$ THEN GOTO 4120
```

In addition, line 4030 would need to be deleted. Not only would this amendment allow a search on the full author's surname but it would also retrieve on any truncation. Thus, items by 'Pritchard' would be retrieved whether the search was made on 'P', or 'Pr', or 'Pri', or 'Prit', through to 'Pritchard'. Note, however, that a search on 'Pri', for instance, would yield not only 'Pritchard' but all names in the data base beginning with 'Pri', eg 'Priestley', or 'Pritt'.

The reader will, no doubt, already have some ideas as to how search routines can be utilized. The possibilities are endless.

APPENDIX – FILES

So far, in the programs described in this text, the data has been included *within* the program. This poses two problems. Firstly, the amount of data that can be processed is, because of computer storage space problems, severely restricted. Secondly, and quite obviously, the processing instructions have to be contained in a single program. These problems can be of great significance, especially when large amounts of data have to be stored, which is often the case in information handling.

The storage capacity of a computer can be measured in terms of 'bits'. Each bit can be thought of as representing a '1' or a '0' (binary mode). It takes 6/8 such bits to store one 'character'.

A microcomputer's memory is usually referred to in terms of 'bytes'. Each byte consists of eight bits and will hold one character. The storage capacity is normally presented as so many 'K', where K is roughly equivalent to one thousand bytes. A 48K memory therefore equals approximately 48,000 bytes, or 48,000 × 8 bits. The memory must hold not only data but also the instructions and various other items required by the computer for efficient operation.

In the cataloguing program described on p67, each catalogue entry contained forty characters. One hundred entries would therefore consist of 4,000 characters, which would require 4K (4,000) bytes of storage. And these were very simple entries! It is clear that it would not take a very large catalogue to overload the 'immediate access' memory capacity.

The answer is to store the data in a separate 'file' in a 'backing', or secondary, store on magnetic tape or magnetic disk. Sections of the data can then be fed into the computer as necessary for processing. Programs can also be stored in this way.

The use of 'files', the name being chosen by analogy with office files, allows far more data to be handled and it also allows the processing of the data using several different programs. One program might be used merely to enter data, another to search the data, another to modify the data, and so on.

110

BASIC is not the best programming language for file handling but most versions have facilities which enable the user to 'WRITE' data on to tape or disk and to 'READ' it from the tape or disk as necessary. A major difficulty is that these facilities are not standardized, the methodology varies widely from computer to computer. Because of this and because this work is intended as an elementary introduction, no detailed explanation of file handling will be given. However, it is necessary to make some general observations about files and their use.

Two statements which may well be encountered, no matter what the version of BASIC, are:

OPEN   as the name implies, this statement is used to open a file;

CLOSE   again, as the name implies, this statement is used to close a file.

Files must always be 'opened' before use and 'closed' after use.

Some computers may not use the OPEN and CLOSE statements but simply call up a file with the statement:

FILES

The file must be named for identification, eg:

OPEN . . . CAT

Between the OPEN statement and the name of the file there may be other details; perhaps a 'logical file number' to be used when 'reading' or 'writing to' a file; perhaps a 'physical device number', eg the cassette drive to be used if there is more than one; and perhaps an 'input/output option', defining whether the file is merely to be 'read' (which prevents it being written on) or 'written', or both 'read and written', eg:

OPEN 1, 1, 0, "CAT"

which means open logical file 1; assign file to cassette 1; open tape for 'read'; look for physical file named 'Cat'. The file would be 'closed' by:

CLOSE 1

111

This is the format that would be used, for instance, on a Commodore Pet microcomputer.

Other microcomputers may adopt a different approach, eg:

```
D$ = CHR$(4)
PRINT D$;  "OPEN CAT"

.  .  .

PRINT D$;  "CLOSE CAT"
```

These statements would be used to open and close files using an Apple microcomputer; they employ a control character D$.

The above examples illustrate just how widely computer instructions for file handling vary. The important thing to note is that *between* the 'OPEN' and 'CLOSE' statements, however formulated, *the principles of programming remain very much the same as those described in this text.*

Some statements, however, may be used in a slightly different way, eg:

PRINT	to write data from the computer to an input/output device such as a disk;
INPUT	to read data from the input/output device to the computer.

READ and WRITE statements may also be used, on some computers, to transfer information to and from files.

The following brief extracts from a program produced at the West Suffolk College of Further Education for the sorting, listing and searching of a periodicals file (reproduced here by kind permission of the Librarian, Robin Shreeve) illustrates that the principles of BASIC programming are constant even if the file handling facilities are not:

```
10    DIM TI$(300),DY$(300) *

 .  .  .

310   HOME : VTAB 12 : PRINT "WELCOME TO THE WEST
      SUFFOLK COLLEGE"
311   PRINT : PRINT : PRINT : HTAB 10 : PRINT
      "PERIODICAL MANAGER"
```

```
. . .
320    PRINT "          OPTIONS"
330    PRINT : PRINT : PRINT
340    PRINT "1       LIST BY TITLE"
350    PRINT "2       LIST BY DEWEY"
360    PRINT "3       SEARCH BY DEWEY"
370    PRINT "4       SEARCH BY TITLE"
380    PRINT "5       ADD A TITLE"
390    PRINT "6       DELETE A TITLE"
400    PRINT "7       EXIT"
410    INPUT "        OPTION? ";U
. . .
420    ON U GOSUB 1000, 2000, 3000, 4000, 5000, 6000, 7000
. . .
3000   REM  **  SEARCH BY  **
3001   REM  **    DEWEY    **
3010   PRINT : PRINT : PRINT : INPUT "DEWEY CODE? ";C$
3020   FOR K = 0 TO J
3030   IF LEFT$ (DY$(K),3) <> C$ THEN 3050
. . .
9000   REM  **  SORT  BY  **.
9001   REM  **    DEWEY    **
9010   FOR K = . . .
9030   IF LEFT$ (DY$(K),DK) <= LEFT$ (DY$(K + 1),DK)
       THEN 9090
9040   A$ = DY$(K)
9070   DY$(K) = DY$(K + 1)
9080   DY$(K + 1) = A$
9090   NEXT
9110   RETURN
. . .
```

This program, apart from being a file handling program, contains other features such as options whether to select v.d.u. screen or printer. The above extracts omit these features

*Note the use of two letters (see p18) for the names of the character variables. A mnemonic facility is thereby provided, ie TI = Title and DY = Dewey.

as well as the file handling routines but the similarities between this program and those described in Part Two of this text are obvious.

One last point should be noted. Files may be of two types: *sequential* or *random access*. In sequential files, such as on magnetic tape, each record is read in sequence one after the other. Such a file only permits *serial* access, where all of the tape preceding an item must be run through before the item is reached. Random access, as on magnetic disk, permits *direct* access to any item of data. The latter is clearly a much faster searching process.

The way in which sequential and random-access files can be processed using BASIC will be explained in the user manual for the particular computer in use.

FINAL NOTE

Having read through this book, you may wish to learn more about other uses of the BASIC language, perhaps the mathematical or graphical possibilities, or you may wish to continue your study of the language to a more advanced level. There are so many books that deal with BASIC that it would be impossible to list them here. Haunt the bookshops and the shops that specialize in computers (the latter often have a better selection of relevant books) and try to find those works which seem to be most suitable for your particular requirement.

Remember, when you pursue your studies, that there is always more than one way to solve a particular problem. There are several different ways, for instance, in which sorting and searching may be done by computer. The programs given in this text are merely illustrative and there is no doubt that the reader will find different, and perhaps better, methods which might have been used. Remember also that the best way to learn is to 'do'. There is no substitute for 'hands on' experience where computer programming is concerned.

If you decide, having worked through this text, that programming is not for you, do not despair; you do not have to be able to program in order to make use of the computer. A whole range of ready-made programs is available to enable the computer to perform an amazing number of operations. Some of this software, as it is called, can be applied to character manipulation. There are, for example, quite a few data base management programs available for a variety of computers. Not all of these are as applicable to library operations as one might at first imagine; shop around, and approach libraries, and other relevant organizations and institutions, in order to ascertain the sort of programs that they are using. Find out whether any software developed in-house might be made available, either as a gift or for purchase.

Where microcomputers are concerned, there is a useful directory of applications in libraries and information retrieval, which lists libraries in the UK which are using microcomputers, indicates the makes of computer in use, and gives details of software. This is: Burton, Paul F *Microcomputer applications in libraries and information retrieval: a directory of users* Leith Nautical College, Edinburgh, 1981.

Periodicals, as well as books, can yield very useful information on microcomputers and programming. There are a great number of these. The DIALOG information retrieval service, which is based in California, now offers (among its many data bases available on-line via remote terminals) a 'Microcomputer index'. This is a subject and abstract guide to articles from over twenty-one microcomputer journals.

Good luck!

INDEX

Entries in capital letters refer to the statements of BASIC.
When a topic is dealt with on several consecutive pages, only the first relevant page number is given.
Italicized page numbers refer to illustrations.

Alphabetical order, sorting
41, 48, 72
Alphanumeric order,
sorting 51
AND logical operator 89,
94
Arrays 47
ASCII character set 42, *44*

Backing stores 14, 110
Bar-code labels 102, *103*
Binary system 7
Bits (binary digits) 110
Books, numbers represent-
ing, issue systems 93, 99
Branching 36, 37
BS 4058 (standard for
flowchart symbols) 63
Bubble sorts 48, 71
Bytes 110

C.p.u. 13
Calculation boxes, flow-
charts 63

Calculations 26
Cataloguing, programs 67
Central processing unit 13
Character strings 18, 39,
75, 104
CHR$ 42
Circulation systems,
programs 91
Classified order, sorting
51, 71
Clearing the screen 50
CLOSE 111
COBOL 8
CLS 50
Colon, use of, separation of
statements with a single
line number 69, 72
Comma, use of, printing
53
Commands 23
Conditions 28
Core (immediate access)
store 13, 110
Counts 29, 68, 92
Cursor, use of 24

DATA 20
Data 13, 20, 78
Data bases 79
Decision boxes, flow-
  charts 63
Decisions 28
DEL(ete) 24
DIM(ension) 47
Direct access 114
Disks 14, 110

Editing 24
END 16
Error detection, invalid
  input 36, 70, 89, 94

Fields 79
FILES 111
Files 79, 110
Fixed fields 79
FLASH 95
Flowcharts 58
  symbols 63
    standards 63
FOR . . . NEXT 29
FORTRAN 8

GOSUB 35
GOTO 28

High-level languages 7
Histograms 31
HOME 50
HTAB 54

IF . . . THEN 28
Immediate access store 13
  110
INPUT 14, 112
  combined with instruc-
    tional message 69
Input 13
118

Input boxes, flowcharts
  63
Interactive programming 8
Invalid input 36, 70, 89,
  94
Issue systems, programs 91

'K' 110
Keyboards 13, 15

Languages, programming 7
LEFT$ 42, 45, 76
LEN 42, 89, 109
LET 26
Library users, numbers
  representing, issue
  systems 93, 99
Light pens 102, 103
Line numbering 16
Lines
  length on screen 52
  number on screen 52
LIST 23
Lists 47
LOAD 23
Logical files 111
Logical operators 70, 74,
  89, 94
Loops 29
  escape routines 40
  nested loops 31, 74
  STEP 74
Low-level languages 7

Magnetic disks 14, 110
Magnetic tapes 14, 110
Memory 14, 110
Menu-driven programs 69
Microcomputers, configur-
  ation 15

MID$ 43, 105
Mnemonics, variable names
  18, 113

Nested loops 31, 74
NEW 23
NEXT 29
NORMAL 96
Numbers, issue systems,
  representing books or
  readers 93, 99
Numerical order, sorting
  51

OLD 23
ON 70
OPEN 111
OR logical operator 70, 74,
  94
Output 13
Output boxes, flowcharts
  63
Overdue notices, issue
  systems 102

Packages, ready-made
  programs 115
PASCAL 8
Periodicals handling,
  programs 112
PRINT 16, 112
Printers 13, *15*, 73
Printing 52
Processing unit 13
Process boxes, flowcharts
  63
Programming languages 7
Programs
  (definition) 14
  names 23

Random access 114
READ 14, 20, 111
Readers, numbers repre-
  senting, issue systems 93,
  99
Records 78
Relational operators 41, 90
REM(arks) 25
Reservations, issue
  systems 94, 102
RESTORE 57
RETURN 35
Return key, use of 22, 24
RIGHT$ 43
Rogue strings 41
RUN 16

SAVE 23
Searching
  by author 75
  by class number 75
  by key word from title
    104
Screens
  length of lines 52
  number of lines 52
  zones 53
  see also Visual display
    units
Secondary stores 14, 110
Semi-colon, use of 53
Sequential files 114
Serial access 114
Software 115
Sorting 41, 48, 71, 72
Statements 14
  more than one after a
    single line number
    69, 72
STEP 74

STOP 28
Storage 13, 14
  capacities 110
String functions 42
Strings 18, 39, 75, 104
STR$ 43
Subscripts 47
Subroutines 35, 70
System commands 23

TAB 54
Tape 14, 110
Terminator boxes, flow-
  charts 63
Truncation 104, 109

V.d.u. 13, *15*
  see also Screens
VAL 45
Variable fields 79
Variables 18
  names 16, 18
Visual display units 13,
  15
  see also Screens
VTAB 54

West Suffolk College of
  Further Education 112
WRITE 111

Zones 53